WHEN I SMITE THE LAND

THE TEN PLAGUES OF EGYPT

RON KNAPP, JR.

DEDICATION

To the wonderful congregation of Antioch Baptist Church
in Greencastle, Indiana, who let me continue preaching
this series even after we were swarmed by flies!

CONTENTS

	Outlines	9
1	The Purpose of the Plagues	23
2	The First Plague	37
3	The Second Plague	53
4	The Third Plague	67
5	The Fourth Plague	79
6	The Fifth Plague	97
7	The Sixth Plague	109
8	The Seventh Plague	123
9	The Eighth Plague	139
10	The Ninth Plague	153
11	The Tenth Plague	163
12	The Passover	179
13	The Conclusion	193
	Bibliography	197
	Illustrations	198

PREFACE

This book is meant to be an encouragement to each of you. I want you to experience all the blessings of God in your life. I want you to rest assured in the knowledge that God loves you and He has a plan for your life. I want you to look at whatever circumstance or situation that comes into your life and be able to say with an unshakeable confidence, "I know that I can do all things, through Christ which strengtheneth me!"(Philippians 4:13)

How am I going to encourage you? I am planning on encouraging you by presenting a study on the plagues that God sent upon Egypt. Maybe you are not so sure that you can find encouragement in rivers of blood, beds with frogs, or hail stones the size of Volkswagens but I assure you that this study will be encouraging.

For those who might be using this book to help prepare for devotionals, Sunday school lessons or sermons, outlines have been included. Many different sources have been used in the development of these sermons and a bibliography has been included. References for illustrations given as part of the sermons are included along with the text. The images of the gods and goddesses are also referenced. All Scriptures are from the King James Version of the Bible.

OUTLINES

THE PURPOSE OF THE PLAGUES

Exodus 5, 6, and 7

I. Before Afterward
   A. Background
   B. Purpose
II. Pre-plague Encounter
   A. Aaron's Rod
   B. Sorcerers' Rods
III. Cobra Goddess
IV. Pharaoh's Response
   A. God Hardens Pharaoh's Heart
   B. Pharaoh Refuses to Hear

THE FIRST PLAGUE

Exodus 7:14-25

I. A Message From the LORD
    A. Moses Sent
    B. Moses Speaks
II. The First Plague
    A. The LORD Acts
    B. Pharaoh Responds
III. Gods and Goddesses of the Nile River

THE SECOND PLAGUE

Exodus 8:1-15

I. The LORD Warns
    A. The Message
    B. The Plague
II. First Reactions
    A. Pharaoh Refuses
    B. Sorcerers Respond
III. Pharaoh Changes His Mind
    A. Pharaoh Calls for Moses
    B. Pharaoh Hardens His Heart
IV. Frog Goddess

THE THIRD PLAGUE

Exodus 8:16-19

I. Without Warning
    A. Stubborn Refusal
    B. Sudden Rebuttal
II. The Plague
    A. The Method
    B. The Lice
III. The Response
    A. The Magicians
    B. The Pharaoh
IV. God of the Earth

THE FOURTH PLAGUE

Exodus 8:20-32

I. Moses Sent to Pharaoh
    A. The LORD Sets the Place
    B. The LORD has a Message
II. The Plague
    A. Mercy is Offered
    B. Judgment is Announced
    C. A Distinction is Made
    D. Not a Coincidence
III. Pharaoh Offers to Compromise
    A. Compromise One
    B. Compromise Two
IV. The Plague Removed
    A. Moses Entreats the LORD
    B. Pharaoh Hardens His Heart
V. Fly Gods or Goddesses

THE FIFTH PLAGUE

Exodus 9:1-7

I. A Warning Issued
    A. The LORD's Message
    B. The LORD's Mercy
        1. The Choice
        2. The Chance
II. The Plague
    A. The Hand of the LORD
    B. The Nature of the Plague
    C. The Distinction
III. The Reports of the Plague
    A. Egypt's Report
    B. Israel's Report
IV. God of Bulls

THE SIXTH PLAGUE

Exodus 9:8-12

I. Without Warning
    A. The LORD Sends
    B. The LORD Commands
II. The Plague
    A. The Plague's Description
    B. The Plague's Sufferers
III. Pharaoh's Reaction
IV. Gods of Health

THE SEVENTH PLAGUE

Exodus 9:13-35

I. The LORD Sends
   A. The Same Message
   B. A Dire Warning
II. The Plague Described
   A. Mercy Extended
   B. Some Believed
III. The Plague Comes
   A. A Grievous Hail
   B. The Destruction
IV. Pharaoh's Reaction
   A. Pharaoh's Request
   B. Moses' Response
V. God and Goddess of Weather

THE EIGHTH PLAGUE

Exodus 10:1-20

I. The Message
    A. The LORD Explains
    B. The Message
II. The Plague
    A. The Announcement
    B. The Compromise
    C. The Locusts
III. Pharaoh's Reaction
    A. Called in Haste
    B. Moses Prays
    C. Pharaoh's Heart
V. God and Goddess of Agriculture

THE NINTH PLAGUE

Exodus 10:21-29

I. The Plague Comes
    A. Without Warning
    B. The Plague Described
    C. The Plague's Extent
    D. The Distinction
    E. Pharaoh Reacts
II. God of the Sun

THE TENTH PLAGUE

Exodus 11:1-10, 12:29-37

I. The LORD's Message to Moses
    A. The Assurance of the LORD
    B. The Blessings of the LORD
II. The LORD's Message to Pharaoh
    A. The Warning
    B. The Distinction
    C. The Refusal
III. The Plague Comes
    A. The Firstborn Die
    B. Pharaoh Reacts
    C. The LORD Delivers
IV. God and Goddess of Children

THE PASSOVER

Exodus 12:1-27

I. Passover Established
    A. Established by the LORD
    B. A New Beginning
II. Specific Instructions
    A. Concerning the Blood
    B. Concerning the Lamb
    C. Concerning the Bread
    D. Concerning the Eating
III. The Specific Promise

THE TEN PLAGUES OF EGYPT

THE PURPOSE OF THE PLAGUES

I. Before Afterward

Exodus 5:1-2

> *And afterward Moses and Aaron went in, and told Pharaoh, Thus saith the LORD God of Israel, Let my people go, that they may hold a feast unto me in the wilderness. [5:2] And Pharaoh said, Who is the LORD, that I should obey his voice to let Israel go? I know not the LORD, neither will I let Israel go.*

A. Background

There are many major elements to understanding the plagues that are wrapped up in the word "afterward".

Rather than trying to include an in-depth study of those events, let me summarize several hundred years of history. Seventy people went into Egypt with Joseph and now they have grown into a large multitude, probably between two and three million people. They were once free people in the land but since the death of Joseph, they have become the slaves of the Egyptians. The Egyptians had become fearful that the number of slaves was growing too large to be controlled. In an attempt to slow the growth of the slave population, the Pharaoh commanded that any male child born to the Hebrews would be cast into the Nile River.

Moses was born during this time but his mother hid him. She made a little basket of reeds and placed the baby inside it. Moses was saved by an Egyptian princess and he grew up in the palace of Pharaoh. One day Moses came upon an Egyptian who was abusing an Israelite. Moses intervened and the Egyptian was killed. Now a wanted man, Moses had to flee from Egypt. It has been many years and the LORD had been preparing Moses for a time when he would return and lead his people out of bondage and into the Promised Land.

Moses offers lots of excuses as to why he could not do what God was calling him to do. Finally, Moses appears before Pharaoh and makes God's command known to him.

Pharaoh looks at Moses and Aaron and states unequivocally that he does not know this God of whom Moses speaks of and he does not have any plans on letting the people of Israel go and worship.

I am not sure what Moses and Aaron expected to come out of this meeting but I am sure that they did not expect it to add to the hardship of their people. Pharaoh decided that the Hebrews must not have enough work to do and he adds to the work that the slaves must produce. This causes the people of Israel to murmur and complain against Moses and Aaron and God.

Exodus 5:20-23

And they met Moses and Aaron, who stood in the way, as they came forth from Pharaoh: [5:21] And they said unto them, The LORD look upon you, and judge; because ye have made our savour to be abhorred in the eyes of Pharaoh, and in the eyes of his servants, to put a sword in their hand to slay us. [5:22] And Moses returned unto the LORD, and said, Lord, wherefore hast thou so evil entreated this people? why is it that thou hast sent me? [5:23] For since I came to Pharaoh to speak in thy name, he hath done evil to this people; neither hast thou delivered thy people at all.

Moses takes this right to the LORD and asks why is this happening? I did what you told me to do and yet it looks to me like you did not fulfill your promise. Pharaoh hates us, the Israelites hate us, and we are in a terrible mess.

B. Purpose

Exodus 6:1-9

Then the LORD said unto Moses, Now shalt thou see what I will do to Pharaoh: for with a strong hand shall he let them go, and with a strong hand shall he drive them out of his land. [6:2] And God spake unto Moses, and said unto him, I am the LORD: [6:3] And I appeared unto Abraham, unto Isaac, and unto Jacob, by the name of God Almighty, but by my name JEHOVAH was I not known to them. [6:4] And I have also established my covenant with them, to give them the land of Canaan, the land of their pilgrimage, wherein they were strangers. [6:5] And I have also heard the groaning of the children of Israel, whom the Egyptians keep in bondage; and I have remembered my covenant. [6:6] Wherefore say unto the children of Israel, I am the LORD, and I will bring you out from under the burdens of the Egyptians, and I will rid you out of their bondage, and I will redeem you with a stretched out arm, and with great judgments: [6:7] And I will take you to me for a people, and I will be to you a God: and ye shall know that I am the LORD your God, which bringeth you out from under the burdens of the Egyptians. [6:8] And I will bring you in unto the land, concerning the which I did swear to give it to Abraham, to Isaac, and. to Jacob; and I will give it you for an heritage: I am the LORD. [6:9] And Moses spake so unto the children of Israel: but they hearkened not unto Moses for anguish of spirit, and for cruel bondage.

As we look in these few verses, we see the purpose of the plagues. Four times in these verses God says, "I am the LORD". This is special. He says Abraham, Isaac, and Jacob knew me as God Almighty but you and Israel are going to know me by my personal name, Jehovah, which means the eternal, self-existent, holy, sin-hating, faithful, covenant keeping, and all powerful God that delivers.

The purpose for the bondage and the persecution and the plagues is to reveal that there is a God and that He is in control. Unlike the gods of Egypt, Jehovah is not a god that is far off and aloof. Jehovah is a God that wants you to know Him personally.

Now you would probably think the people of Israel would be excited by this news but they were not. They looked at their circumstances, bondage, and cruel treatment and they refused to believe that God would be able to deliver them.

Rejected by the Israelites Moses probably thinks that this is the end of the mission but look what God tells him to do.

Exodus 6:29-30

That the LORD spake unto Moses, saying, I am the LORD: speak thou unto Pharaoh king of Egypt all that I say unto thee. [6:30] And Moses said before the LORD, Behold, I am of uncircumcised lips, and how shall Pharaoh hearken unto me?

God says, go and deliver the message to Pharaoh. I have some things that I want you to say to him. Can you almost hear Moses protesting? One of the excuses Moses gave for not going to Pharaoh earlier was that he was slow of speech. Many believe he probably stuttered. You... you...you...want... want... want... me to do what?! Wait a minute God, the Israelites won't listen to me and they hate me. Pharaoh has already made it clear he does not like me or them and he has made life even more miserable for us. You want me to go back and make him even angrier?

Exodus 7:1-7

And the LORD said unto Moses, See, I have made thee a god to Pharaoh: and Aaron thy brother shall be thy prophet. [7:2] Thou shalt speak all that I command thee: and Aaron thy brother shall speak unto Pharaoh, that he send the children of Israel out of his land. [7:3] And I will harden Pharaoh's heart, and multiply my signs and my wonders in the land of Egypt. [7:4] But Pharaoh shall not hearken unto you, that I may lay my hand upon Egypt, and bring forth mine armies, and my people the children of Israel, out of the land of Egypt by great judgments. [7:5] And the Egyptians shall know that I am the LORD, when I stretch forth mine hand upon Egypt, and bring out the children of Israel from among them. [7:6] And Moses and Aaron did as the LORD commanded them, so did they. [7:7] And Moses was fourscore years old, and Aaron fourscore and three years old, when they spake unto Pharaoh.

In these verses, God expands the purpose of what He is going to do. Not only will Israel, Moses, and Aaron know and see the power of God but so will Pharaoh and so will the Egyptians. God says, Moses right now it may seem that Pharaoh isn't paying attention to you but I have made you like a god in his eyes. Pharaoh is going to revere you and respect you in ways that he would treat a high dignitary or a god. He may act like he is not listening to Aaron but I have made Aaron like a prophet.

Pharaoh will not be able to say, "Who is the LORD" or "I know not the LORD." God says, I am going to harden his heart and I am going to do many miracles and signs and wonders but Pharaoh will still not listen to you. But when I stretch forth my hand, when I send forth my armies, then will the Egyptians know that I am the LORD.

These two young men set out to do what God has commanded them. Moses is 80 and Aaron is 83 years old. I thank God for our silver saints! Seeing faithful Christians coming to the house of the Lord into their 70's, 80's and 90's is a true blessing. You are never too old for God to be done with you!

II. Pre-plague Encounter

A. Aaron's Rod

Exodus 7:8-13

And the LORD spake unto Moses and unto Aaron, saying, [7:9] When Pharaoh shall speak unto you, saying, Shew a miracle for you: then thou shalt say unto Aaron, Take thy rod, and cast it before Pharaoh, and it shall become a serpent. [7:10] And

Moses and Aaron went in unto Pharaoh, and they did so as the LORD had commanded: and Aaron cast down his rod before Pharaoh, and before his servants, and it became a serpent. [7:11] Then Pharaoh also called the wise men and the sorcerers: now the magicians of Egypt, they also did in like manner with their enchantments. [7:12] For they cast down every man his rod, and they became serpents: but Aaron's rod swallowed up their rods. [7:13] And he hardened Pharaoh's heart, that he hearkened not unto them; as the LORD had said.

Now the Lord told Moses and Aaron that Pharaoh would speak to them and Pharaoh was going to demand a sign or a miracle. If you are speaking for this LORD, God Almighty, prove it! Show me something miraculous.

God said when he asks for a miracle, tell Aaron to throw his rod down and it shall become a serpent. Now this rod of Aaron's is going to be a symbol of the power and presence of God all during the time that the Israelites wander through the wilderness. But up to this point it has just been a common walking stick. Now just imagine Moses', Aaron's, and Pharaoh's surprise when Aaron cast that rod on the floor and it became a serpent.

The word used for serpent carries with it the idea of a great monster. God did not tell Moses and Aaron how large the serpent was going to be and I wonder if it didn't scare them just a little bit when God revealed His power through this ordinary object. I wonder if Pharaoh jumped up on his throne.

B. Sorcerers' Rods

The Bible does tell us that Pharaoh calls for his wise men and his sorcerers. When these men come in before the Pharaoh they also produce serpents. The Scripture says that every man's rod became a serpent. We are not told how many serpents were slithering around on the floor but it would be reasonable to assume that there are probably six or more serpents in the throne room.

The Scriptures tell us that Aaron's rod swallowed up their rods. This is an amazing event. This is not something that happens in nature. A snake may eat another snake but no snake is going to eat two or more snakes at one time. If I am correct, there are at least six snakes slithering around the throne room of Pharaoh and Aaron's rod ate them all.

III. The Cobra Goddess

Now this is a pre-plague encounter but this is where God begins to assert that the god's of Pharaoh were not really gods at all. If you look at the history of ancient Egypt you will find that they worshipped many gods.

It is said that the Egyptians of this time worshipped over eighty different deities. They would have only been rivaled by India in their polytheism. Like the Indian's, they worshipped a large number of animals and anthropomorphic beings as gods. The animals considered to be sacred included many insects like the scarab and locust; many mammals like the lion, ox, ram, wolf, dog, and cat; many fowls like the falcon, and vulture; many

31

aquatic creatures like fish, frogs, and crocodiles; and very prominently we find the worship of the cobra.

I cannot prove that Aaron's rod turned into a giant cobra but I believe it is quite likely because the cobra was sacred and represented Lower Egypt and kingship.

The Uraeus is a head piece of the pharaohs which depicted an Egyptian spitting cobra in an upright position (Figure 1). This cobra was the symbol of sovereignty, royalty, deity, and divine authority in ancient Egypt.

Figure 1

The cobra also represents the goddess Wadjet, one of the earliest of Egyptian deities. Wadjet began as a goddess of a city but became the protector of all of Lower Egypt. The headdress encircled the head of the Pharaoh indicating her protection to the ruler and the land.

Wadjet was sacred to all classes of people in Egypt. She was a fertility goddess protecting the Nile River and women during childbirth. It was believed that she had the power to purify the motives of men and that she was able to grant humility to men. It was said that all men would learn from Wadjet. Some men would learn wisdom and some would learn woe but all would learn something.

So here in this pre-plague encounter between Moses and Pharaoh we see that God Almighty, the LORD, Jehovah is showing Pharaoh that his goddess, Wadjet, the cobra, is not a god at all.

IV. Pharaoh's Response

A. God Hardens Pharaoh's Heart

Exodus 7:13

> ***And he hardened Pharaoh's heart, that he hearkened not unto them; as the LORD had said.***

First, God hardened Pharaoh's heart. Many Bible Scholars struggle with the thought that God would harden a man's heart. But this is certainly the judgment that is being sent to Pharaoh. He has seen the miracle of God Almighty, the LORD, Jehovah and faced with a choice to obey the one true God or to continue to worship and pursue false gods, he chooses the false gods. This is a sad phrase that will be repeated many times as we look at the plagues. Seven different times we will read that God hardens Pharaoh's heart and four times we will read that Pharaoh hardens his own heart.

One Bible commentator put it this way, the same sun that melts the ice, hardens the clay. Some will face circumstances and turn from God and others facing the same crisis will have their hearts soften and turn to God.

B. Pharaoh Refuses to Hear

Secondly, Pharaoh harkened not unto them. What?! Are you kidding me?! This rod just turned into a giant cobra. This rod just ate all the other rods in this room. This rod, right here, you saw what just happened and yet your heart is hardened and you will not listen?!

Pharaoh has had more than one encounter with Moses and Aaron at this point. God has been merciful and God has been patient. In this pre-plague encounter God is giving Pharaoh an opportunity to repent, to listen, to soften his heart, and acknowledge the one true God.

God is about to stretch forth His hand and smite Egypt but there have been no judgments, yet. However, with every subsequent encounter between Moses and Pharaoh the stakes get higher and higher. These encounters are coming with the purpose that Israel and the Egyptians, Moses and Pharaoh will all know that the LORD alone is God.

QUESTIONS

1. Looking back in your life, can you see a warning or a miracle that the LORD performed to get your attention?

2. How do you respond to the knowledge that the LORD wants you to know Him personally?

3. How do you respond to the idea that the LORD hardened Pharaoh's heart?

4. What might you do to keep your heart softened to the will of the LORD?

5. How will you overcome giving excuses instead of obeying the LORD?

THE FIRST PLAGUE

Exodus 7:14-25

In the pre-plague encounter between Moses and Pharaoh, God challenged and defeated Wadjet, the protector of the kings, the protector of the Nile, and the protector of women. God is using the symbols of the gods of Egypt to show that He is the one true God and this was the first strike in the battle to determine who will be God.

This miracle did not persuade Pharaoh to let the people go or cause him to believe upon the name of the LORD. Pharaoh's refusal to believe God will lead directly to the plagues. We tend to focus upon the devastation of the plagues and we overlook the goodness of the LORD in the plagues.

There is a message of encouragement in the plagues because with each subsequent plague we see the mercy of God, the longsuffering of God, and His ability to deliver His people while judging His enemies.

Exodus 7:14-21

And the LORD said unto Moses, Pharaoh's heart is hardened, he refuseth to let the people go. [7:15] Get thee unto Pharaoh in the morning; lo, he goeth out unto the water; and thou shalt stand by the river's brink against he come; and the rod which was turned to a serpent shalt thou take in thine hand. [7:16] And thou shalt say unto him, The LORD God of the Hebrews hath sent me unto thee, saying, Let my people go, that they may serve me in the wilderness: and, behold, hitherto thou wouldest not hear. [7:17] Thus saith the LORD, In this thou shalt know that I am the LORD: behold, I will smite with the rod that is in mine hand upon the waters which are in the river, and they shall be turned to blood. [7:18] And the fish that is in the river shall die, and the river shall stink; and the Egyptians shall lothe to drink of the water of the river. [7:19] And the LORD spake unto Moses, Say unto Aaron, Take thy rod, and stretch out thine hand upon the waters of Egypt, upon their streams, upon their rivers, and upon their ponds, and upon all their pools of water, that they may become blood; and that there may be blood throughout all the land of Egypt, both in vessels of wood, and in vessels of stone. [7:20] And Moses and Aaron did so, as the LORD commanded; and he lifted up the rod, and smote the waters that were in the river, in the sight of Pharaoh, and in the sight of his servants; and all the waters that were in the river were turned to blood. [7:21] And the fish that was in the river died; and the river stank, and the Egyptians could not drink of the water of the river; and there was blood throughout all the land of Egypt.

I. A Message From the LORD

A. Moses Sent

As we read this passage, we see that although Pharaoh would not hear the first attempts of the LORD, Moses is sent to him yet again. There is a difference in the settings of the meetings. The first audiences were before Pharaoh in the throne room. This meeting is at the river side. Many speculate that Pharaoh had determined that he would simply ignore Moses' requests for an audience and thus rid himself of the trouble.

Pharaoh's heart is hardened but the LORD will not be ignored. He has a message for Pharaoh and it must be delivered. Moses is not judged as a failure or success based upon the reception of the message. He is told ahead of time that Pharaoh will not listen (Exodus 7:4) but the LORD still commands Moses to deliver the message.

Notice that the LORD knew where Pharaoh would be on the morrow. He holds all men's lives in His hands and knows what men are thinking and men are doing. Pharaoh goes to the Nile River. This is not an uncommon thing for men to do. Often people who live near a river will go out and walk along its banks. Pharaoh is not out on a power walk for his daily exercise or a pleasure walk to see the sights of the river. He went down to the Nile River to worship it and to present his daily sacrifice to it.

Also notice that Moses is commanded to take the rod, the very rod that had turned into a serpent, with him to the Nile River. This rod represents the power and presence of God. Moses is not to take just any rod that he finds along the way. Maybe there is a newer style of the rod that is easier to carry. Maybe there is another rod that all the other Israelites are using. Maybe there is a rod that is made from a newly discovered material.

I believe that we can make a comparison to using the same rod to using the same Bible. This Bible, the KJV, represents the power and the presence of God. There is an alphabet soup of Bibles out there today. You can get any combination of letters you want. They are based on another text. They are easier to carry because they have taken out many of the words and verses. Many of the other churches are using them. God told Moses, you take the same rod and get down to the Nile to meet the Pharaoh.

B. Moses Speaks

The LORD has given Moses a message to deliver to Pharaoh. It is the same message as the first meeting. "Let my people go that they may serve me in the wilderness." Now I believe the fact that the message does not change is significant. Today many churches want to take and hide the message of the Gospel. They want to change to make it more palatable. Let's not talk about sin, or hell, or damnation. But the LORD God of the Hebrews says deliver the same message to Pharaoh. I am the LORD God of the Hebrews. I demand that you let my people go to serve me in the wilderness.

Notice the next phrase, hitherto thou wouldest not hear. God has told Moses to remind Pharaoh that he has not listened yet. I don't think that is a recommended method in closing a deal. Remind them that they haven't listened so far. God said, remind him of the purpose of these meetings and the miracles. He has not listened yet but did you see the purpose of these encounters is repeated in verse 17?

Exodus 7:17

Thus saith the LORD, In this thou shalt know that I am the LORD:

In all that God is doing, He is displaying that He is the one true God. If Pharaoh would hear and receive the message, he would not need to suffer through the plagues. If he would have acknowledged that the LORD is God, and repented of his sins, he would not need to go through these terrible plagues. Pharaoh's problem is that he has many other gods to whom he is beholden. He would rather serve them than serve the LORD.

II. The First Plague

A. The LORD Acts

And now we see the first plague upon the general population of the Egyptians. The water of the Nile River will be turned to blood, all the fish shall die, the river shall stink, and the people will not be able to drink it. The Scriptures say that the water actually became blood. It was not just a red color but was changed or turned to blood. An obvious connection can be made with the fact that the Egyptians had stained the water of the Nile with the blood of the Hebrew children and now God turns its water to blood as a judgment against them.

The plague was immediate. As soon as the rod touched the river the water within it turned to blood. But the effect of this plague was not just upon the water around Pharaoh at the morning worship site. The water was turned to blood in the river, in the streams, in the ponds, in the pools and in the vessels of earth and the vessels of stone. The pre-plague encounters really only had an impact or impression upon Pharaoh and those who witnessed them but this plague now touches the life of every Egyptian. Their water was turned to blood. The fish in the river, streams, ponds and pools died. The land stank. There is no denying that something terrible and supernatural had happened.

Notice that the LORD has commanded that Aaron take the rod, which had been turned into the serpent, and in the presence of Pharaoh and his servants he is to smite the water with it. When Moses and Aaron first came to Pharaoh probably most of the people would not have been able to tell you who they were but now when Pharaoh and his servants see them, they know them. I would imagine that many of them can now recognize the rod that Aaron carries, too. At first it was just another stick but now it represents the power and presence of the LORD God of the Hebrews.

When Moses commands Aaron to stretch out his rod and smite the water and at that very moment all those people see the water turn to blood, do you think it made an impression upon them? I believe that it did!

B. Pharaoh Responds

Exodus 7:22-25

And the magicians of Egypt did so with their enchantments: and Pharaoh's heart was hardened, neither did he hearken unto them; as the LORD had said. [7:23] And Pharaoh turned and went into his house, neither did he set his heart to this also. [7:24] And all the Egyptians digged round about the river for water to drink; for they could not drink of the water of the river. [7:25] And seven days were fulfilled, after that the LORD had smitten the river.

Although many of the people were probably impressed and gave some thought to the power of the LORD God of the Hebrews, Pharaoh did not. It does not make any sense to me but the sorcerers do just what they did before. They also turned water into blood. If all the water is blood and you had water that wasn't blood, would you make it blood? If I were Pharaoh, I would have demanded that the magicians turn the blood back to water. That would have given sufficient cause to dismiss the miracle wrought at Moses' command but instead they copied the miracle.

The Scriptures record that Pharaoh's heart was hardened. Pharaoh turned and went back to his house unimpressed with the message from the LORD. You might expect that Pharaoh would go back to the palace and call his wise men and counselors together to discuss what had happened. The Scriptures says that Pharaoh went into his house and neither did he set his heart to this also.

He just turned his back and ignored this miraculous sign that God had provided to him. For seven days the water remains blood. For seven days his people are digging about trying to find water to drink. For seven days the stink of the river filled the land and yet for seven days the Pharaoh did not set his heart to this.

III. Nile River Gods and Goddesses

Why would Pharaoh not even consider this plague? The pre-plague encounter was a challenge to the Egyptian god Wadjet but this first plague against the general population of Egypt was an attack upon multiple gods related to the worship of the Nile River.

I have included a list of five of the Nile River gods and goddesses. There are multiple spellings of each god or goddess' name making them somewhat difficult to trace. Added to the confusion is that the history or genealogy of the gods and goddesses has changed overtime.

Khnum was one of the earliest of the Egyptian
gods. He was originally depicted as the provider of the
Nile River having a vessel from which the river flowed.
The Nile River was seen as the source of life to the
Egyptians and over time Khnum morphed into a creator
god. It was believed that he created the bodies of human
children upon a potter's wheel and would place them into
the wombs of mothers-to-be. In Figure 2, Khnum
fashions a child upon the wheel and the god Thoth,
standing behind Khnum, numbers the days of the child's
life.

Figure 2

Hapi is another of the Nile River gods. He was also said to be the god that provided the Nile River and the fish and birds of its marshes to the Egyptian people. He was also a fertility god bringing life to the land through the yearly flooding of the Nile River. In Figure 3, Hapi is depicted as two gods. The left side of the image is the god of the Southern Nile River and the right side of the image is the god of the Northern Nile River.

Figure 3

   Osiris is the god of the underworld who sees to it that the dead are judged. He is considered to be the god of the resurrection and of new life. He is closely associated with the changing of seasons. He was betrayed by friends and placed in a box which was cast into the Nile River. It was commonly believed that it was his blood that flowed in the Nile that brought life to Egypt. In Figure 4, Osiris is seen on a bier with wheat growing from him.

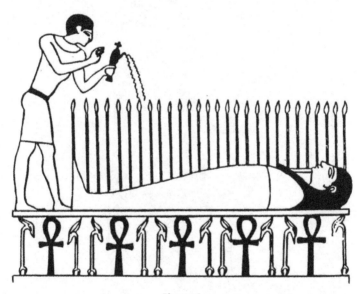

Figure 4

Tauret is the goddess who is depicted as a pregnant hippopotamus. She is another fertility goddess symbolizing the rebirth and regeneration associated with the Nile River. In Figure 5, she is seen standing on her hind legs and holding the key of life.

Figure 5

Nu is said to be the oldest of the ancient Egyptian gods. He is said to be the father of the sun god, Re. The Egyptians believed he was the source of everything in the world. In Figure 6, he is seen holding up a boat filled with Egyptians with a scarab holding up the sun.

Figure 6

The purpose of this plague is the same as the former encounters between Pharaoh and Moses. This plague was meant to reveal to Pharaoh that the LORD Jehovah is the one true God.

All that Pharaoh has been taught and all that he believes is being challenged by the message of the LORD. I believe that the message of the LORD has that same power today.

We do not worship the gods and goddesses of the Egyptians but we have a multitude of substitutes. The world will tell you that you need possessions to be happy. You need a good job, a nice house, a beautiful wife or a handsome husband and then you will be prepared for anything life can throw at you. Can you see that these things are little more than replacements for the gods of the Egyptians?

QUESTIONS

1. Are you faithful at delivering the message of God?

2. If God is the same yesterday, today, and forever, why do you think there are so many different messages being given by the church?

3. Has there been a time when you experienced the mercy of God even when you had first rejected the message?

4. How can you be sure to not ignore the working of God in your life?

5. Are there gods in your life that you need to reject?

THE SECOND PLAGUE

Exodus 8:1-15

The first plague was not really directed at the Nile River. It was only performed against the Nile River because the Nile River represented the gods of Egypt. Pharaoh had gone to the river to offer worship to these gods. When the LORD performed this miracle, He was proving that the Egyptian gods were not gods at all. They could not protect the river and they cannot protect the people or Pharaoh. It is important to remember the plagues were meant to show Pharaoh and Egypt that the LORD is God and Jehovah is His name.

Exodus 8:1-7

> *And the LORD spake unto Moses, Go unto Pharaoh, and say unto him, Thus saith the LORD, Let my people go, that they may serve me. [8:2] And if thou refuse to let them go, behold, I will smite all thy borders with frogs: [8:3] And the river shall bring forth frogs abundantly, which shall go up and come into thine house, and into thy bedchamber, and upon thy bed, and into the house of thy servants, and upon thy people, and into thine ovens, and into thy kneadingtroughs: [8:4] And the frogs shall come up both on thee, and upon thy people, and upon all thy servants. [8:5] And the LORD spake unto Moses, Say unto Aaron, Stretch forth thine hand with thy rod over the streams, over the rivers, and over the ponds, and cause frogs to come up upon the land of Egypt. [8:6] And Aaron stretched out his hand over the waters of Egypt; and the frogs came up, and covered the land of Egypt. [8:7] And the magicians did so with their enchantments, and brought up frogs upon the land of Egypt.*

I. The Lord Warns

A. The Message

Once again we see that the message from the LORD is the same. Thus saith the LORD, let my people go, that they may serve me. Remember what the word LORD represents. This is the personal name of God, Jehovah. Jehovah means the eternal, holy, self-existent, sin-hating, faithful, covenant keeping, and all powerful God. When Moses speaks to Pharaoh he is to say, "Thus sayeth the LORD." Pharaoh has ignored the LORD. He has said, "I do not know the LORD" and asked, "Who is the LORD?" The LORD has started to reveal Himself to Pharaoh and with each passing plague Pharaoh is moving closer and closer to the eternal judgment of the LORD. The message is meant to remind Pharaoh that the plagues are happening at the command of the LORD.

Many scholars believe that it has been seven days since Moses has come before Pharaoh. No doubt Moses has been praying and seeking what God would have him do. Perhaps Moses thought surely, today Pharaoh will call for me. He will want the river restored. He will see that the LORD, He is God! But one day passes, another day passes and another and Pharaoh does not call for Moses. But the LORD is gracious and patient and in wrath and judgment He still remembers mercy. So after seven days, the river is restored and life starts to get back to normal.

Is that not how we live our lives? A crisis or tragedy or decision point is reached in our lives. What are we going to do about _____? We are experiencing it. We see it. We smell it. We taste it. It consumes our conversations and our thoughts. We think we cannot go on or that we do not know what to do. After suffering through the initial trauma and shock, we begin to recover and think everything is all right now. We decide that wasn't from the LORD. It was a coincidence. It was my emotions. It was just a fluke.

Pharaoh sees the river restored and he thinks it was all just a coincidence. He scoffs; the LORD did not do this. Yet the message is the same. It is from the LORD and He is demanding Pharaoh's attention.

B. The Plague

The LORD tells Moses that if Pharaoh refuses to listen to the message, a second plague will come upon the land. It will be a plague of frogs! The river that was blood, where all the fish were dead, that stank and was undrinkable will bring forth frogs in abundance. Pharaoh, the frogs will be in your palace. They will be in your bed. These frogs will be in your servant's homes. These frogs will be in the homes of your people. These frogs will be in the royal ovens and in the royal kneading troughs. These frogs will be upon you, your people, and your servants.

Now let's be reasonable about this. Are frogs something to be afraid of? Even children can catch frogs. Frogs don't bite. Frogs don't sting. Frogs are not huge. Frogs are not ferocious. When was the last time you saw a horror movie called The Attack of the Killer Frogs?

Can you picture the look on Pharaoh's face? What?! Did you just say that this all powerful, holy, self-existent, blah, blah, blah, God of yours is going to plague me with frogs? That's ridiculous. I will not let you go for fear of frogs. Frogs, Oh my, not frogs! I am so afraid, not!

The LORD could have threatened Pharaoh with lions, or tigers or (dramatic pause) wolves. He could have used bears, vultures or any number of other creatures known for fierceness but the LORD chose to use frogs.

All the earth is His creation and all the earth can be used to bring glory to the LORD. Even the smallest of His creatures can be obedient and can have an eternal influence for good.

II. First Reactions

A. Pharaoh Refuses

The LORD is still being merciful and gracious to Pharaoh. He says that if you refuse, then I will smite the land with this plague. Do you realize what this implies? The LORD is implying that if Pharaoh would listen, he would not have to endure this plague. It would not have to come upon him and his people. If Pharaoh would acknowledge the LORD and let the Israelites go, this plague could be avoided. This message is given as a warning to Pharaoh but it displays God's mercy, too. Do not ignore the LORD! If you ignore Him, you do so at your own peril.

Ezekiel 33:11

Say unto them, As I live, saith the Lord GOD, I have no pleasure in the death of the wicked; but that the wicked turn from his way and live: turn ye, turn ye from your evil ways; for why will ye die, O house of Israel?

The purpose of the plagues was to reveal that the LORD is the one true God. The purpose is not to destroy Pharaoh but to glorify the LORD. It is to bring about repentance in the life of Pharaoh.

This same offer is being made to us! If we will receive the message, if we will accept the LORD as Saviour of our lives, the path of our lives will be changed. We will no longer be going down the path of death and destruction but we will be on the path of righteousness and life. We will have troubles but we will no longer be under the condemnation of our sins.

Although a way to avoid the plague was offered to Pharaoh, he refuses to hear the message. The LORD spoke to Moses and Moses spoke to Aaron. Aaron took the rod, the one that became a serpent, the one that turned the water into blood and he stretches it forth over the waters again. Immediately, the frogs began to come up out of the water. Remember, the rod is not magical. It represents the power and presence of God. When Pharaoh saw that rod and his sorcerers saw that rod, it reminded them that the LORD worked through it.

I believe that Moses and Aaron also had come to appreciate that rod. Pharaoh and his people feared it but Moses and Aaron were in awe. It is difficult for those who are not saved to look at this Bible and see the goodness of the LORD. They read of sin and they read of judgment and they read of righteous living and they think I cannot do that, I cannot give this sin up, I cannot be the things it says I should be and many turn away from it. As a Christian, I look into this Bible and I see forgiveness of sin, I read of redemption, I read of the promises of God and I think I cannot do anything but what it says and I want to know more and more about the Word of the LORD.

B. The Sorcerers Respond

When Aaron stretched forth the rod, immediately the frogs began to come up out of the rivers and streams and ponds and pools. The frogs covered the land and filled all the houses. Frogs are everywhere.

Pharaoh calls his sorcerers and they were able to make the waters bring forth frogs, too! That does not seem like much of an answer to me. In the last plague, they took water and turned it to blood but they could not take the blood and turn it to water. Here they cause frogs to come up out of the water but they could not make them go back into the water.

III. Pharaoh Changes His Mind

Exodus 8:8-14

Then Pharaoh called for Moses and Aaron, and said, Intreat the LORD, that he may take away the frogs from me, and from my people; and I will let the people go, that they may do sacrifice unto the LORD. [8:9] And Moses said unto Pharaoh, Glory over me: when shall I intreat for thee, and for thy servants, and for thy people, to destroy the frogs from thee and thy houses, that they may remain in the river only? [8:10] And he said, To morrow. And he said, Be it according to thy word: that thou mayest know that there is none like unto the LORD our God. [8:11] And the frogs shall depart from thee, and from thy houses, and from thy servants, and from thy people; they shall remain in the river only. [8:12] And Moses and Aaron went

59

out from Pharaoh: and Moses cried unto the LORD because of the frogs which he had brought against Pharaoh. [8:13] And the LORD did according to the word of Moses; and the frogs died out of the houses, out of the villages, and out of the fields. [8:14] And they gathered them together upon heaps: and the land stank.

A. Pharaoh Calls for Moses

Here is the first instance where Pharaoh calls for Moses and Aaron. He scoffed at the thought that frogs would be used as a plague against him. Is that all you got? Frogs! Bring them on, I am not afraid! But now he sends for Moses and Aaron and he says, "Intreat the LORD, that he may take away the frogs from me, and from my people; and I will let the people go, that they may do sacrifice unto the LORD."

You may not think much of this verse but it is loaded with an amazing admission on the part of Pharaoh. He once said, who is the LORD, and I know not the LORD. But now he acknowledges that there is a LORD. He acknowledges that it was the LORD that sent the frogs and that it will have to be the LORD that takes them away. Pharaoh acknowledged that this plague was the work of the LORD.

What does Moses do? Moses says, Pharaoh, you pick the time that you want the frogs to leave. You take the glory from me and put it upon yourself. Moses puts a high confidence in God. He tells Pharaoh, you set the time that you want the frogs to be destroyed and I will pray to the LORD and it will happen at that time. Pharaoh asks that the frogs be removed on the morrow.

Many sermons have been titled "One more night with the Frogs" and many have speculated why Pharaoh chose tomorrow for the frogs to be removed. I do not know. It is possible that he thought it too great a work to be accomplished right away and therefore he sets it for the next day. Instead of speculating on why Pharaoh chose the time, I want to consider the importance of letting Pharaoh set the time.

The LORD is going to show Pharaoh that it is not the alignment of the stars or coincidence or natural circumstances that have brought forth these frogs and it will not be any of those things which remove them either. Pharaoh sets the time and Moses prays that the LORD will act so that Pharaoh will know that the LORD is the one true God.

The LORD answered Moses and all the frogs died. The Scripture says that the people piled them in heaps and that the land once again stank. The frogs were dead but the decaying heaps served as a reminder that they had been sent and destroyed by the LORD.

B. Pharaoh Hardens His Heart

Exodus 8:15

But when Pharaoh saw that there was respite, he hardened his heart, and hearkened not unto them; as the LORD had said.

With this plague, Pharaoh acknowledged the LORD. With this plague, Pharaoh has promised that he would let the people go to serve the LORD. With this plague, the wrath and mercy of the LORD have been fully revealed. Still we see that as soon as the plague was removed, Pharaoh hardened his heart.

IV. Frog Goddess

The first plague was against the various gods and goddesses of the Nile River but this plague seems to be against one specific goddess named Heqet. She is depicted as being in the form of a frog or as a woman with a frog head. She is often associated with the god Khnum. He would create the child upon the potter's wheel and she would give the child life in the mother's womb. Heqet is circled in Figure 7.

She was also seen as a fertility goddess. The Egyptians would see the frogs coming forth from the Nile River each year as a sign of blessings and fruitfulness.

Figure 7

The people believed that if there were plenty of frogs, there would be plenty of crops. She was also a goddess of childbirth. Many women would wear an amulet or bracelet with her depiction to protect them during their pregnancy. It is commonly believed that the midwives in ancient Egypt were called ministers of Heqet. But like the last plague the LORD showed that there is no God but Jehovah.

Pharaoh tried to ignore the first plague. He turned and went into his palace but there was no escaping this plague. Frogs were everywhere and there was no rest for anyone until Moses prayed.

QUESTIONS

1. Do you find it easy to forget the LORD after the crisis has past?

2. Has the LORD used something small to get your attention?

3. How quickly would you ask the LORD to remove what troubles you?

4. Why is it important to note that Moses did not ridicule Pharaoh?

5. How earnestly do you pray for others when they request it?

THE THIRD PLAGUE

Exodus 8:16-19

Two of the plagues have passed and although Pharaoh has acknowledged them to be the work of the LORD he is still unwilling to let Israel go into the wilderness to worship. Instead, we read that Pharaoh hardened his own heart. His stubborn refusal to acknowledge the LORD brings about the third plague but unlike the first two this one comes without a warning.

Exodus 8:16-19

And the LORD said unto Moses, Say unto Aaron, Stretch out thy rod, and smite the dust of the

land, that it may become lice throughout all the land of Egypt. [8:17] And they did so; for Aaron stretched out his hand with his rod, and smote the dust of the earth, and it became lice in man, and in beast; all the dust of the land became lice throughout all the land of Egypt. [8:18] And the magicians did so with their enchantments to bring forth lice, but they could not: so there were lice upon man, and upon beast.
[8:19] Then the magicians said unto Pharaoh, This is the finger of God: and Pharaoh's heart was hardened, and he hearkened not unto them; as the LORD had said.

I. Without Warning

A. Stubborn Refusal

I have repeated that the purpose of all of the plagues is to bring Pharaoh, the Egyptians, Moses and the Israelites to recognize and acknowledge that it is the LORD who is the one true God. The LORD has been merciful and gracious as He begins dealing with Pharaoh. Pharaoh is offended by hearing that an unknown god is making a demand of him. At the conclusion of the last plague, he had to acknowledge that it was the LORD alone that controlled the plague. Sadly, even when he acknowledged the LORD, Pharaoh still refused to hearken to His call.

When Pharaoh saw that there was a respite from the previous plague, he hardened his heart. He is in a very dangerous situation. He knows the message is from the LORD. He knows what the LORD is requiring of him. Yet Pharaoh's devotion to his own way of living will not allow him to come to the LORD and be saved. When the plague of frogs is lifted, he determines that he will not let the LORD's people go.

B. Sudden Rebuttal

No time frame is given to us but it would seem that immediately upon Pharaoh's refusal to let the people go a new plague comes upon the land. Unlike the first plagues, this plague comes without warning. The LORD did not send Moses to Pharaoh to give him warning or even to tell him what the plague was going to be.

Hebrew scholars divide the plagues into three groups of threes followed by the final plague. In each of the three groups, the first two plagues come with a warning but the third does not.

The LORD has been dealing with Pharaoh and has been merciful. Pharaoh did not need to suffer the plague of frogs but he refused to listen to the LORD. Pharaoh has presumed upon the goodness and graciousness of the LORD.

We may be tempted to think that this is unfair of the LORD but Pharaoh has been given fair warning. Pharaoh knows what the LORD wants and he knows that to refuse is to suffer further plagues.

Do not think that the LORD is obligated to send you a little postcard that says, By the way, next week, I will be sending this into your life, if you continue to refuse Me. Signed, The LORD.

We are all prone to presume upon the goodness of the LORD. Maybe you can relate to this modern day parable:

During a flood, a certain man became trapped in his home. He began to pray asking that God would rescue him. His neighbor, who owned a huge four-wheeled drive vehicle offered to give him a ride. The man refused saying, I am waiting for God to save me.

The water continued to rise and the man had to climb up on the roof of the house. Another neighbor came by in a boat and offered to take the man to safety. Once again the man replied, "I am waiting for God to save me."

The water continued to rise and the man continued to pray. All the while he believed that he would be saved by God. Now a helicopter flies by and begins to lower a ladder to take the man off of the roof. The man refused, shouting back to the crew that he was waiting for God to save him. The waters continued to rise and the man drowned.

In heaven, he asked God why He did not save him. God replied, "I sent a truck, a boat, and a helicopter and you refused them all!"

Someone might say, well if this thing would happen or that thing would happen, then I would listen, then I would obey. That is an admission that they know they are not doing what the LORD would have them to do but they are making excuses to continue in their sin. The

LORD is not obligated to give you any more warnings before judgment comes.

II. The Plague

A. The Method

Moses is to tell Aaron to take the rod, the same rod that turned into a serpent, the same rod that turned the waters into blood, and the same rod that brought forth the frogs, and smite the dust of the land. The rod is the symbol of the power and presence of the LORD. Aaron is to take and smite the dust of the land with the rod. The LORD continues to display His power and presence through the same old rod.

I like the thought that the Bible I hold in my hand is the same Bible that my grandfather read and that our founding fathers read. What a blessing to know that the LORD who inspired men to write it has also been able to preserve it. I don't need a new version of a 1978 book that was promoted as correcting all the mistakes of the past. Give me the old Bible! I want the same Bible that brought the great revivals of the past and can be traced back to ninety-five percent of all existent manuscripts.

But while the rod is the same this plague is different from the previous plagues. The first two plagues were upon the Nile River and the waters of Egypt but now this plague comes upon the land of Egypt. Many believe that the LORD wanted to show Pharaoh that He was not merely the LORD over the rivers and waters but he was also the LORD over the land. The LORD is the eternal, holy, self-existent, sin-hating, faithful, covenant keeping, and all powerful God. He created and controls the entire universe. The LORD can cause the waters and the lands to bring forth blessings but at His command they can also bring forth judgment.

B. The Lice

When Aaron strikes the dust of the land with the rod, the dust of all the land of Egypt becomes lice. One word for that is EWWW!

Now that seems like a simple sentence but this thought of lice has stirred up quite a bit of controversy. Some think it was lice, like we know today. Others think it was gnats, others mosquitos, others ticks or sand fleas, while others say it might have been something not known before or since. I do not care what you think they were, whether lice, gnats, mosquitos, ticks, sand fleas or some unknown creature it is still EWWW!

Most scholars do agree that these creatures were very small, likened to the size of dust specks and that they were very troublesome. The Egyptians could not keep these creatures from getting on them or in their homes or on their animals. These lice were everywhere on man and beast.

The frogs were small and Pharaoh summarily dismissed them as a threat but after a day he relented and asked for Moses to pray that they be removed. This plague is of creatures the size of dust specks and yet they were as much trouble, if not more than the frogs.

THE TEN PLAGUES OF EGYPT

Around our house, I have seen an interesting little insect. It is extremely small, grayish black and comes in the thousands. I cannot stop them from going wherever they want but they seem to have no desire to attach themselves to anything that is alive. These insects are the size of dust specks but can you imagine how uncomfortable they could make your life if they were parasites? These small parasitic lice infected everyone and every beast in Egypt.

III. The Response

A. The Magicians

Remember that Moses and Aaron did not announce that this plague was about to come upon Egypt. There was no word from Moses saying this was going to happen but when the magicians saw what was going on, they knew it was the LORD.

The magicians tried to bring forth the lice by their enchantments but they could not. I still find these magicians of Pharaoh to be very interesting. When confronted with the miracle of the serpent, they made more serpents. When confronted with the Nile River being made blood, they also made water into blood. When confronted with a plague of frogs, they also brought forth frogs. Here, when confronted with this plague of lice, they try to create more lice.

This is how the world looks at the miraculous workings of the LORD. They try to explain Him away. Using faulty logic, they summarily dismiss the fact that the

LORD is revealing Himself to them and calling them to acknowledge Him as LORD and Saviour.

As we studied the previous plague, Pharaoh acknowledge that the frogs came by the power of the LORD and were removed by the power of the LORD. Here the magicians said this is the finger of God. They have also acknowledged that there is a LORD and He is the one in control of this plague.

You might be tempted to think that this is what we would call the salvation point for the magicians but it is not. Although Pharaoh admitted that the LORD performed the last plague and removed it, he was not saved. The magicians are willing to admit that this was done by a divine power, but they are also not saved.

The Bible teaches us that simply believing that there is a God is not enough. God is calling us to acknowledge Him and then obey Him.

James 2:17-20

Even so faith, if it hath not works, is dead, being alone. [2:18] Yea, a man may say, Thou hast faith, and I have works: shew me thy faith without thy works, and I will shew thee my faith by my works. [2:19] Thou believest that there is one God; thou doest well: the devils also believe, and tremble. [2:20] But wilt thou know, O vain man, that faith without works is dead?

Pharaoh and the magicians were to the point that they had to acknowledge that there was indeed a God but they had not yet surrendered themselves to follow Him.

B. The Pharaoh

Once again we read that Pharaoh's heart was hardened and that he would not hearken unto them. It would seem that at this point the magicians were the ones that Pharaoh would not hearken to because Moses and Aaron had not come to speak to him. His own counselors come to him and tell him this is of God and yet he will not hear. Previously, Moses and Aaron have come and he will not hear. The plagues have come and he will not hear. The last plague was removed at the very time that he requested it to be and yet he will not hear.

IV. God of Earth

This particular plague is generally thought to be against the Egyptian god of the earth named Geb. He was known as a fertility god and was thought to be in control of everything on, in, or under the earth. The worship of Geb would have been interrupted as the lice coming forth out of the dust would spoil the sacrifices and interfere with the priests as they tried to perform their ceremonies.

Figure 8

QUESTIONS

1. What do you think about the fact that God is not obligated to warn you before He sends judgment?

2. How have you presumed upon the goodness of the LORD?

3. Has there been a time in your life that non-believers have pointed out that the LORD was working?

4. How will you move beyond acknowledging God to obeying Him?

5. Is there something you are waiting to see or do before you serve the LORD?

WHEN I SMITE THE LAND

THE FOURTH PLAGUE

Exodus 8:20-32

The plagues have gotten progressively worse and have affected more and more people. And yet, in the plagues, we still can see the goodness, kindness, forgiveness, and mercy of the LORD. As we have progressed through the plagues, we have found that Pharaoh went from asking, "Who is the LORD?" to acknowledging that the LORD was the one that was in control of the plagues. In the third plague, Pharaoh's magicians came to him and acknowledged that the plague of lice was "the finger of God."

But as of yet neither Pharaoh nor the magicians were willing to obey the LORD. Even in their obstinacy the LORD is merciful. Remember that the Scripture tells us that the Egyptian people would not need to suffer, if Pharaoh would let the Hebrew people go. This is an offer of mercy before the plague comes. Also recall that when Pharaoh called and asked Moses to pray that the plague be removed, the LORD answered the prayer of Moses. This is mercy after the plague.

While you and I are tempted to say "Three strikes and you're out", the LORD is not willing that any should perish.

2 Peter 3:9

The Lord is not slack concerning his promise, as some men count slackness; but is longsuffering to us-ward, not willing that any should perish, but that all should come to repentance.

The LORD is long suffering toward us! He wants us to acknowledge Him as LORD and then He wants us to serve Him.

Pharaoh is not willing to submit to the LORD. Following each plague, we have read that the heart of Pharaoh was hardened. The plagues that revealed the power and mercy of the LORD have not softened Pharaoh's heart. This is the choice of Pharaoh. We can look at what the LORD is doing and say, I see and I repent or we can say, I do not believe it and I will have my own way.

I. Moses Sent to Pharaoh

Exodus 8:20

And the LORD said unto Moses, Rise up early in the morning, and stand before Pharaoh; lo, he cometh forth to the water; and say unto him, Thus saith the LORD, Let my people go, that they may serve me.

A. The LORD Sets the Place

Once again we see that the LORD speaks to Moses and He sends him to speak to Pharaoh. The LORD tells Moses to go and stand before Pharaoh. Pharaoh is up early. Many believe that he is headed to the Nile River as an act of worship and some even believe it was to open a religious festival for the people of Egypt. No matter, the LORD says go and stand before him. This does not merely mean to be there as Pharaoh passes but it means to stand against him, to oppose him, or to confront him.

Moses, one of the slaves, an outcast and one of Pharaoh's least favorite people, is told to go and stand against Pharaoh. I don't think this is such an easy thing to do. At least it is not nearly as easy as we read it.

The LORD does not promise that everything we are going to be called to do will be easy. Some things we are called to do are joyous and others are difficult but we must be faithful! Moses goes and stands before Pharaoh.

B. The LORD has a Message

You already know the message. "Let my people go, that they may serve me." There is but one message. It is from the LORD, the eternal, self-existent, holy, sin-hating, faithful, covenant keeping, and all powerful God. He has heard the cries of His people and he is going to bring deliverance to them.

The LORD wants you to know that He does exist and that there is no other god like Him. He is the one true God. He holds your life in His hands. He has a message for you! He wants you to be set free from your sins so that you may serve Him.

II. The Plague

Exodus 8:21-24

Else, if thou wilt not let my people go, behold, I will send swarms of flies upon thee, and upon thy servants, and upon thy people, and into thy houses: and the houses of the Egyptians shall be full of swarms of flies, and also the ground whereon they are. [8:22] And I will sever in that day the land of Goshen, in which my people dwell, that no swarms of flies shall be there; to the end thou mayest know that I am the LORD in the midst of the earth. [8:23] And I will put a division between my people and thy people: to morrow shall this sign be. [8:24] And the LORD did so; and there came a grievous swarm of flies into the house of Pharaoh, and into his servants' houses, and into all the land of Egypt: the land was corrupted by reason of the swarm of flies.

A. Mercy is Offered

We tend to focus on the negative side of what is being said. If you and I paraphrase what these verses are saying, we would probably say it like this: Pharaoh let my people go or suffer the consequences. Right? But couldn't these verses be just as easily paraphrased to say: Pharaoh be blessed by acknowledging and obeying the LORD? You see here in this little word "else" we are seeing the mercy of the LORD.

B. Judgment is Announced

The LORD says, be blessed or be judged. The plague that is being announced is that of swarms of flies. Commentators have argued that the translators of the Bible added "of flies" in error. I know they added it but I believe they have faithfully preserved the Word of God.

Flies are not uncommon in Egypt. In fact the flies of Egypt were described in detail by travelers. The following paragraph is from Keil and Delitzsch Commentary on the Old Testament via E-Sword.

> *"These insects [Dog Flies] are described by Philo and many travellers as a very severe scourge (vid., Hengstenberg ut sup. p. 113). They are much more numerous and annoying than the gnats; and when enraged, they fasten themselves upon the human body, especially upon the edges of the eyelids, and become a dreadful plague."*

Dog Flies or Black Flies are known to attack people, pets, and agricultural animals, too. These bites are extremely painful to both man and animal. If the flies are hungry, they will continue to pursue their meal even after being swatted at numerous times.

One kayaker gave this account of his encounter with Black Flies.
(http://www.winnipesaukee.com/forums/showthread.php?p=126014)

"I kayaked from our house to Loon Island, in the middle of Moultonborough Bay. Beautiful day. As I got close to the island, I was suddenly engulfed in black flies. They must have been sitting on the island just waiting for something to eat. They got in my ears, nostrils, eyes and on every possible patch of exposed skin. Horrible!

I thought of jumping out of the kayak to escape them, but then I would have to swim back ... out of the question. I paddled back as fast as I could. The further I got from the island, the fewer flies attacked, but a cloud of 'em followed me back, hounding me. Tough to paddle and swat flies at the same time. I was actually lumpy from the bites for a while."

This plague of flies in Egypt was going to be so thick! These flies would be upon Pharaoh, his servants, and his people. These flies were going to be in the houses of Pharaoh, his servants, and his people. These flies would be covering the ground. The swarms of flies were going to be everywhere.

C. A Distinction is Made

Well, almost everywhere. Until this plague, we are not told specifically that the Hebrew people were spared from the plagues that came upon Egypt. I will not enter into that debate but it is certain that with this plague a distinction is being made between the Egyptians and the Israelites.

Perhaps Pharaoh is still tempted to believe that what was happening is not really of the LORD. Perhaps he had a counselor or group of counselors that had devised a theory that explained the origins of these plagues without needing the LORD. I know that might be hard to believe but let's just say that it is plausible. So these scientists, I mean counselors, tell Pharaoh that somehow, something got in the water and turned it to blood. This blood turned into frogs and the lice came from the dead frogs. And then the flies have come from the dead lice.

Perhaps Pharaoh has noticed that these plagues were coming on the Israelites as well as the Egyptians and he thinks this cannot be the hand of their God because they are suffering, too.

Whatever the reason, the LORD tells Moses to tell Pharaoh that these flies are going to be grievous to the Egyptians but they will not be on the Israelites.

D. Not a Coincidence

The LORD is going to take control of the swarms of flies and they will only be able to go where He would have them go. The LORD also set the time that this plague would begin "To morrow shall this sign be". This is no coincidence; this is the hand of the LORD.

Pharaoh will not need to look anywhere else for an explanation for these grievous swarms of flies. There is only one explanation and that is the LORD is revealing Himself to Pharaoh, to Egypt, to Moses, and to Israel. This plague comes just as the LORD had said.

III. Pharaoh Offers to Compromise

Exodus 8:25-28

And Pharaoh called for Moses and for Aaron, and said, Go ye, sacrifice to your God in the land. [8:26] And Moses said, It is not meet so to do; for we shall sacrifice the abomination of the Egyptians to the LORD our God: lo, shall we sacrifice the abomination of the Egyptians before their eyes, and will they not stone us? [8:27] We will go three days' journey into the wilderness, and sacrifice to the LORD our God, as he shall command us. [8:28] And Pharaoh said, I will let you go, that ye may sacrifice to the LORD your God in the wilderness; only ye shall not go very far away: intreat for me.

A. Compromise One

Pharaoh calls for Moses and Aaron and he tells them to go and to sacrifice unto the LORD but notice that he places a stipulation upon the worship. He says go and sacrifice but do it here in the land of Egypt. He is willing to tolerate their religion to a point. Go and sacrifice but do it here.

Moses tells Pharaoh that this is unacceptable to the LORD and it would also be unacceptable to the Egyptians. We have seen in recent times how the Muslim population riots over perceived slights to their "prophet" and their "holy" book. Death threats were issued over a cartoon. A mob killed Christians over a rumor that the Koran was disrespected. Could you imagine how the Egyptians would react to see the Israelites sacrificing an animal that the Egyptians worshipped?

Moses says, we will not and cannot offer our sacrifices here. We will go three days journey as the LORD has commanded us and there we will offer our sacrifices.

B. Compromise Two

Pharaoh relents and tells Moses that he will let him go into the wilderness to sacrifice to the LORD but notice what he says, "Only ye shall not go very far away." Pharaoh says all right you can go. You can go into the wilderness. You can offer sacrifices. Do all that you need to but don't go too far.

These are the same compromises that Satan offers to Christians today. But if we are to offer spiritual sacrifices to the LORD we must:

Separate ourselves from the wicked and profane of this world. We cannot have fellowship both with the Father of lights and with the works of darkness, both with Christ and with Belial.

We must separate ourselves from the distractions of this world. Matthew Henry said Israel cannot keep the feast of the Lord among the brick-kilns or among the flesh-pots of Egypt. I don't know about you but I find work can distract me from serving the LORD. I find that pleasures and comfort can distract me from serving the LORD. Moses says no we must go into the wilderness.

We must separate ourselves unto the LORD. Notice Moses says, "We will sacrifice as the LORD shall command us, and not otherwise." There can be no compromise. We must follow the commands of the LORD.

We must repent and turn from our sins. We must leave them far behind. Pharaoh says go but don't go too far and that is what Satan calls to us as Christians to do also. Okay, quit doing this sin but let's not be too rash. You might want to come back to it. Satan says let's not be a fanatic. Let's not be too serious about this serving God. As a Christian, we must separate ourselves from sins.

We would do well to remember the old saying, "Sin will take you farther than you want to go, cost you more than you are willing to pay, and keep you longer than you are willing to stay." James tells us that lust bringeth forth sin and sin, when it is finished, bringeth forth death. Our only hope is to leave sin far behind.

IV. The Plague Removed

Exodus 8:29-32

> *And Moses said, Behold, I go out from thee, and I will intreat the LORD that the swarms of flies may depart from Pharaoh, from his servants, and from his people, to morrow: but let not Pharaoh deal deceitfully any more in not letting the people go to sacrifice to the LORD. [8:30] And Moses went out from Pharaoh, and intreated the LORD. [8:31] And the LORD did according to the word of Moses; and he removed the swarms of flies from Pharaoh, from his servants, and from his people; there remained not one. [8:32] And Pharaoh hardened his heart at this time also, neither would he let the people go.*

A. Moses Entreats the LORD

At Pharaoh's request, Moses asked the LORD to remove the plague of the swarms of flies. Pharaoh has not been honest up to this point but Moses is still willing to pray for Him. He also gives Pharaoh a warning, do not deal deceitfully.

Many do not like thinking that the LORD would have messengers to stand against what is popular or what is common place but the LORD sends Moses and Moses confronts sin, even in the life of Pharaoh.

B. Pharaoh Hardens His Heart

Moses leaves the presence of Pharaoh and entreats the LORD for him. The LORD hears and removes the plague of the swarm of flies. And once again we read these sad words, Pharaoh hardened his heart.

V. Fly Gods or Goddesses

The Egyptians worshipped many gods and goddesses and it is commonly reported that one of those goddesses was named Uatchit. She was said to be depicted as a woman with a fly's head. According to E. A. Wallis Budge, the author of, The Gods of Egypt, Volume I and II, this is a mistake. Uatchit is generally depicted as a snake goddess and in one instance was said to take the form of a shrew mouse but she is not known as a fly (Figure 9).

Other commentators believe the reference to flies being supplied by the translators could mean flying insects like the scarab or Egyptian Dung Beetle represented by the god Khepri (Figure 10). Khepri is also often misidentified as having a fly's head.

Figure 9

Figure 10

Although these two gods are not necessarily fly gods, the Egyptians did have a belief that flies protected them from disease. Some Egyptian stone amulets that have been found with the depiction of flies date back to 3500 BC. Other artifacts believed to be used in religious rituals, dating between 2690 and 1650 BC, including "magic wands" made of hippopotamus ivory which have been found engraved with images of the fly.

It is well documented that between 1550-1070 BC there was an honor given to soldiers who exhibited valor or bravery in the field of battle, known as the flies of valor. Currently, the Egyptian Museum of Cairo has on display a gold chain with three pendants in the form of 'flies of valour' that was found in the tomb of Queen Ahhotep I (Figure 11).

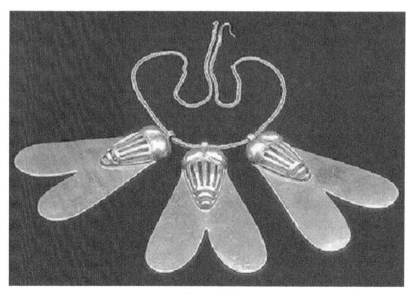

Figure 11

The LORD has revealed to Pharaoh that there is only one God and his name is Jehovah. He is the creator and sustainer of life. He controls the Nile River, the frogs, the lice, and even the flies. He has revealed himself to Pharaoh and Pharaoh must make a decision. Receive the LORD and be blessed or reject the LORD and be judged.

QUESTIONS

1. Can you name a time when you were thankful for the patience of the LORD?

2. How do you respond when confronted with a message you do not want to hear?

3. Do you believe that the LORD can make a distinction between Christians and the world?

4. How will you guard against the compromises that the world offers to Christianity?

5. Would you be as willing as Moses to pray for Pharaoh?

THE FIFTH PLAGUE

Exodus 9:1-7

Then the LORD said unto Moses, Go in unto Pharaoh, and tell him, Thus saith the LORD God of the Hebrews, Let my people go, that they may serve me. [9:2] For if thou refuse to let them go, and wilt hold them still, [9:3] Behold, the hand of the LORD is upon thy cattle which is in the field, upon the horses, upon the asses, upon the camels, upon the oxen, and upon the sheep: there shall be a very grievous murrain. [9:4] And the LORD shall sever between the cattle of Israel and the cattle of Egypt: and there shall nothing die of all that is the children's of Israel. [9:5] And the LORD appointed a set time, saying, To morrow the LORD shall do this thing in the land. [9:6] And the LORD did that thing on the morrow, and all the cattle of Egypt died: but of the cattle of the children of Israel died not one. [9:7] And Pharaoh sent, and, behold, there was not one of the cattle of the Israelites dead. And the heart of Pharaoh was hardened, and he did not let the people go.

I. A Warning Issued

A. The LORD's Message

I would believe that you know what the message of the LORD is by this time but I will repeat it because it is recorded in the Scriptures. The message is let my people go that they may serve me. This is the message that the LORD tells Moses to deliver to Pharaoh time and time again. Pharaoh has refused to hear it. Pharaoh has lied about receiving it. Pharaoh has stubbornly and obstinately refused to hear and obey this message. But the LORD tells Moses to go and take this message to Pharaoh once again.

We, too, have been given a message to deliver to the world. The message is that they can be free from the bondage of their sin. There is a way that they can serve the LORD. They can choose to serve the LORD or they can refuse. But what is our obligation to those who do not know the LORD? We are to go and tell them that they can be free from their bondage. What if they have refused before? What if they have lied about it before? What if their heart seems to be hardened against the LORD? What are we to do? We are to take the same message. We are to deliver it in a loving way. We are to be patient. We are to be kind. But we have no other message.

This is a battle to see whose will is going to stand. Pharaoh has pitted himself against the LORD. Pharaoh knows what the will of the LORD is but he continues to fight against it. The Old Testament contains six verses that describe the LORD as being jealous. Let's consider just one of them.

Exodus 20:5

Thou shalt not bow down thyself to them, nor serve them: for I the LORD thy God am a jealous God,

Now this is not a crazed jealousy like we are tempted to think of today. This is a righteous jealousy. The LORD is the creator, deliverer, sustainer, and protector of all that you are and all that you have. He is not willing to merely be one of the gods in your life. He wants to be the one and only God in your life because He is the eternal, self-existent, holy, sin-hating, covenant-keeping, and all powerful God. Look at how much he loves His people. He is working to deliver them from bondage but at the same time Pharaoh can be delivered. However, Pharaoh must make the choice. He will either be blessed by obeying the LORD or he will be judged by refusing to obey.

B. The LORD's Mercy

Although we see that the LORD loves His people and has a righteous jealousy over them, we also see that the LORD is merciful. Here in verse 2 and verse 5, we

find the mercy of the LORD is revealed yet again to
Pharaoh.

Exodus 9:2 ; 5

*[9:2] For if thou refuse to let them go, and wilt
hold them still,*

*[9:5] And the LORD appointed a set time,
saying, To morrow the LORD shall do this thing in
the land.*

It is unclear exactly how much time passes between
this encounter and the end of the last plague. Some
speculate it was the same day or perhaps no later than the
following day. But no matter when it was we see that the
LORD is still willing to extend mercy to Pharaoh. Pharaoh
has a choice and Pharaoh has a chance.

1. The Choice

The word "if" implies this is a choice. If he would
choose to obey the LORD, he would not need to suffer.
But if he refuses, he will be judged. Moses cannot make
the choice for Pharaoh. The counselors of Egypt cannot
make the choice for Pharaoh. This is a choice that he as an
individual must make.

He can let them go or he can hold them still. This is
a picture of a tightening grip. The LORD says this is what
I want and this is what I demand but Pharaoh says no.
Instead, Pharaoh tightens his grip saying that this is what I
want and I will not release it.

I am reminded of something called a monkey trap. This is a trap to capture small monkeys and is still used by people today. The trap is generally a gourd that is staked to the ground. It has a hole cut into it just wide enough for a monkey to stick its empty hand into. Some type of bait is placed inside the gourd. The monkey reaches for the bait and because it cannot get his hand back out of the trap with bait in his hand, he is captured. The trap works because the monkey will not let go!

Pharaoh could be free but because he refuses to let the Hebrews go and because he continues to tighten his grip, he will be judged. It is his choice.

2. The Chance

Verse 5 also shows us the mercy of the LORD. The LORD could have sent this plague immediately but instead, the LORD says this plague will come tomorrow. Pharaoh has the rest of the day to think about this coming plague. Pharaoh goes home that night and over dinner he is thinking about the plague that is to come. He goes in to watch Egyptian TV or read the Cairo newspaper. He is remembering the former plagues and thinking about the plague that is to come. When he lays his head down on his pillow that night, he is thinking about the coming plague.

Perhaps you have had a time like that in your life. Perhaps you found it completely miserable. You had a choice to make and a chance to make it. I will tell you that I believe that is an example of the mercy of the LORD. The plague is not going to come until tomorrow and you have a choice to make and a chance to stop the coming judgment. The question is will you release your grip so that you can be freed from the monkey trap?

II. The Plague

A. The Hand of the LORD

This plague is not brought about through the rod of Aaron. This plague is credited directly to the hand of the LORD. It is possible that, at first, Pharaoh and the magicians thought Moses and Aaron were just clever sorcerers. Perhaps they thought that somehow the rod of Aaron had some magic powers in it. But you will remember that with the plague of lice the magicians came and told Pharaoh this is the finger of God. Well, if the finger of God brought forth the lice in all the land, this plague will be determined to be the hand of the LORD.

Although Pharaoh might want to write these plagues off as a coincidence, there will be no denying that this is the hand of the LORD.

B. The Nature of the Plague

This plague will come by the hand of the LORD and it will be against the cattle, horses, asses, camels, oxen, and sheep. What is this plague? It will be grievous murrain. So what does that mean?

A murrain is an infectious and fatal disease generally among cattle. This is not something unknown to the Egyptians for they have faced such fatal and infectious diseases before and since but this will be clearly seen as the hand of the LORD because it will start exactly when the

LORD had declared it and this will be more extensive and severe than any general outbreak.

The symptoms are described as a hanging down and swelling of the head, abundance of gum in the eyes, rattling in the throat, difficulty of breathing, palpitation of the heart, staggering, a hot breath, and a shining tongue.

This would be worse than the mad cow disease outbreak in the 1990s when 4.4 million cattle were destroyed in Europe. The hand of the LORD is against the wealth of Egypt. Not every animal in Egypt is killed but millions die. Each of these animals are representative of the wealth of Egypt. There would be no Egyptian that was not affected by this plague. No matter whether they owned any animals or not, they would suffer.

I think of it like gasoline prices, when gas goes up everything goes up. Wool prices go up because the sheep die. Agricultural prices go up because the oxen used in the fields die. Travel costs go up because the camels die. They might even start charging for a second bag of luggage. The cost of other goods brought into Egypt would go up because the asses have died. The horses, one of Egypt's valuable exports to the world at that time, die and the national economy suffers. Do not forget that the cattle, worshipped by the Egyptians, die.

C. The Distinction

But the LORD places a distinction between the Egyptians and the Israelites. While multitudes of these animals are dying in Egypt, none of the livestock belonging to the Israelites will die. This is an amazing miracle. Although the cattle of Israel breathed in the same air, drank of the same water, and fed in the same pastures, they did not have the murrain as the cattle of Egypt.

There is a lesson for us here. The LORD will keep us from some of the troubles, trials, and plagues of this world because we belong to Him. There are two purposes for this distinction.

- The LORD intended to show the Israelites that they were special to Him and that He was able to deliver, protect, and sustain them.

- The LORD intended to show Pharaoh that He is the LORD and Jehovah is His name. Pharaoh is not dealing with Moses and Aaron. He is dealing with the LORD.

The Scriptures tell us that the LORD did just as He had said and just when He had said it.

III. The Reports of the Plague

A. Egypt's Report

Undoubtedly, reports start pouring in from all over Egypt. Cattle are dying. Horses are dying. Asses are dying. Camels are dying. Oxen are dying. Sheep are dying. Imagine the panic among the people. Imagine the sense of horror and loss they must be feeling. Pharaoh sitting upon his throne, hearing report after report, jumps to his feet and says, send someone to the land of Goshen where the

Israelites dwell. I want a report! What is happening in Goshen?!

You know why he wanted to know what was going on in Goshen? If they were affected by the murrain, then there is no God! It was just a coincidence! He must know how are the Israelites affected?

B. Israel's Report

The report comes back and behold - that means shock and surprise, you are not going to believe this! - Not one of the cattle of the Israelites had died. Not one of them. This is truly the hand of the LORD. Still we read that Pharaoh hardened his heart and would not let the people go.

IV. Bull God

In Egypt the cattle, especially the bulls, were worshipped. Apis is the bull god (Figure 12, next page). A bull that matched specific markings would be selected from the herd and brought to the temple. This bull was given a harem of cows. When the bull died, it was mourned over as though a Pharaoh had died. These bulls would be buried in elaborate religious ceremonies.

During the celebration of the feast of Apis, an oxen with special markings would be selected from the herd to be sacrificed. The oxen would be doused in wine and then its throat was cut. The meat of the oxen would be eaten but the head was thrown into Nile River. The Egyptians considered Apis to be a powerful god but their god was no match for the LORD.

Figure 12

QUESTIONS

1. How has God's mercy been revealed in your life through choices?

2. If you were given the chance to think about coming judgment, would you react differently than Pharaoh?

3. Do you believe that God can strike at the wealth of people to get their attention?

4. Is it important to you to see that God makes a distinction between the Egyptians and Hebrews in this plague?

5. How will you ensure that wealth will not become an idol in your life?

THE SIXTH PLAGUE

Exodus 9:8-12

And the LORD said unto Moses and unto Aaron, Take to you handfuls of ashes of the furnace, and let Moses sprinkle it toward the heaven in the sight of Pharaoh. [9:9] And it shall become small dust in all the land of Egypt, and shall be a boil breaking forth with blains upon man, and upon beast, throughout all the land of Egypt. [9:10] And they took ashes of the furnace, and stood before Pharaoh; and Moses sprinkled it up toward heaven; and it became a boil breaking forth with blains upon man, and upon beast. [9:11] And the magicians could not stand before Moses because of the boils; for the boil

was upon the magicians, and upon all the Egyptians.
[9:12] And the LORD hardened the heart of Pharaoh,
and he hearkened not unto them; as the LORD had
spoken unto Moses.

I. Without Warning

A. The LORD Sends

The plagues have gotten more and more severe.
When we studied the third plague, I pointed out that many
Hebrew scholars divide the plagues into three sets of
three, with the final plague standing alone. The pattern
that emerges is that within each set of plagues, the LORD
sends Moses and Aaron to give Pharaoh warning of the
judgment that is to come with the first two plagues of the
set but the third plague comes without warning. This is the
sixth plague and it comes without any specific warning.

It is also important for us to remember that
beginning with the fourth plague the LORD has made a
distinction between the Egyptians and the Hebrews. The
Egyptians were afflicted by the swarms of flies but the
Israelites were not. The Egyptian's cattle and livestock
were afflicted by the murrain but the Israelites' cattle and
livestock were not. This is not a promise that the LORD's
people will never suffer. Experience tells us that the
LORD's people, while living in this world, may suffer
some of the troubles that those who reject the LORD
suffer but by His grace, we will not suffer all that they
suffer.

We are not given any time frame for the onset of
this plague. The plague of the murrain, where multitudes

of the Egyptian livestock have died, is passed. Pharaoh has hardened his heart and has determined that he will not let the LORD's people go that they may serve the LORD.

Was it days or was it hours later that this plague begins? I do not know. It could be that as soon as Pharaoh has made his intentions clear to harden his heart against the LORD that the LORD sends Moses. It could be, in mercy, the LORD gives Pharaoh a day or more to contemplate what he will do.

The LORD deals with us as individuals and He deals with each situation individually. Perhaps one time we need to be confronted immediately, but at another time we need to have some time to contemplate the consequences of our actions. Just because one way works for you today, does not mean that it will work for you tomorrow.

I find this to be very encouraging. Believe it or not there have been times when I have hardened my heart against the message of the LORD. Some people probably thought that the LORD should strike me with a lightning bolt, or give up on me or just write me off. But the LORD looked upon me as an individual. He looked upon me with compassion. He dealt with me as an individual even when I was obstinate and rebellious against Him. At times, the LORD may send judgment but even then He tailors it to me individually and to each situation individually.

This example also stands as a warning to each of us. Just because the LORD does not send punishment immediately, does not mean that we have somehow escaped being punished for our sins. The Bible tells us that the LORD will not be mocked. He has promised to judge sin.

2 Peter 3:9

The Lord is not slack concerning his promise, as some men count slackness; but is longsuffering to us-ward, not willing that any should perish, but that all should come to repentance.

B. The LORD Commands

Moses and Aaron are commanded by the LORD to take two handfuls of ashes from the furnaces. The furnace being spoken of here is most likely the furnaces that the Israelites were forced to labor over for the Egyptians. You will remember that the Israelites were baking the bricks that were being used to build Egypt. For the Israelites, this was a hard labor and an oppressive labor. But these bricks represented the power and strength of Egypt.

So it is rather ironic that the LORD commands Moses and Aaron to both take two handfuls of the ashes from the furnaces that are building Egypt and use those ashes to bring a plague upon the Egyptians.

The LORD has commanded them to sprinkle the ashes toward heaven. I get a picture in my head of cleaning out a fire place. When I take that ash out of the fire place and put it in the bucket, I have to work so it does not fill the room with ash. When I take it out of the house and dump that bucket, I have to be sure that I am not standing downwind. That ash is light and it will be carried on the wind and cover me, if I am not careful. The ashes that Moses and Aaron carry are light and powdery like that, too.

Notice also that the LORD has commanded them to do this in the sight of Pharaoh. I wonder if Pharaoh was downwind. It does not matter, I am just wondering. Downwind or not, Pharaoh sees Moses and Aaron toss the ashes into the air. This was done so that when this plague comes upon the Egyptians, Pharaoh will know that it has come at the hand of the LORD.

II. The Plague

A. The Plague's Description

The LORD has told Moses and Aaron that these four handfuls of ashes will become a dust throughout all the land of Egypt and the LORD describes the results of this dust.

The Scriptures say it will become a boil breaking forth with blains. Now when I read that I think that sounds bad and I don't want it but when I studied this out, I really decided that I did not want it. The ashes are going to create a burning, an inflammation in the skin, and that burning will turn to a blister or a boil. The boils will be breaking forth, this means they are going to be like a flower garden in the spring! The boils are going to spread and blossom all over the body. But these boils are not just going to rise up on the body, they are going to rise up and then explode or erupt – that is what is meant by blains. I think to say this would be an uncomfortable health condition would be an understatement.

113

This is very reminiscent of what is called Nile-blisters. Nile blisters are a rash that comes out in innumerable little pimples upon the skin. They produce a burning or pricking sensation at their first appearance. In a short time they turn into small, round, and thickly-crowded blisters.

Another possible explanation is skin anthrax. This condition is described as a black, burning abscess, and some believe this is a better fit because of the sprinkling of the soot of the furnace. You can search skin anthrax on the web and find some very disturbing images of what this plague may have looked like.

B. The Plague's Sufferers

The Scriptures tell us that this plague will be upon both man and beast. This is significant. As I said earlier, each of the plagues has become more severe. This is the first plague that has been inflicted upon the physical bodies of the Egyptians. No doubt they have been afflicted by the Nile being turned to blood, the frogs in the houses, the lice upon all men, the swarms of flies, and the death of the livestock.

Now the health of the people of Egypt is directly impacted by the plague. Now I must caution you to not jump to conclusions. If someone is suffering hardships economically, emotionally, physically, or in whatever category you would place them, it does not mean that they are being judged by the LORD. But in this case, there is no doubt. The people of Egypt are suffering because the hand of the LORD is against them.

It may seem unfair. Why are they suffering, if the Pharaoh is the one that will not let the Israelites go? The people of the land suffer because of the choices that their leaders make. It is true of any nation, and it is true in any time. The Egyptians suffer the plague of boils because of their leadership's refusal to obey the LORD.

The common people suffered and notice the magicians have returned to the narrative. They are also afflicted by the boils. They could not stand before Moses and Aaron because of the boils. These are the greatest sorcerers in the land. These are the confidants of Pharaoh. Yet they cannot keep themselves from suffering the effects of the boils.

The Scriptures tell us that this plague was upon all the Egyptians. I fully believe that even Pharaoh was afflicted. Can you imagine everywhere that Pharaoh would turn he would be confronted with the evidence that there is one LORD and Jehovah is His name. Everywhere he would turn he would be reminded of that scene where Moses and Aaron threw those handfuls of ash into the air. Everywhere he turned he would hear those words, let my people go, that they may serve me.

Unlike the previous plagues, he could not simply retreat to the palace and hide from the evidence. His advisors were afflicted. His family was afflicted and he was afflicted. He could not look at his reflection without seeing the consequence of his rebellion. He could not look at his arms or hands or legs or feet without seeing the evidence of the plague against him.

III. Pharaoh's Reaction

Surely, this would be the turning point. Pharaoh has been close in some of the previous plagues. You will remember he called for Moses and Aaron and asked them to pray and ask the LORD to remove the plague of frogs. You will also remember that Pharaoh was willing to offer a compromise. He said worship the LORD but he added some stipulations that were unacceptable to the LORD. How could Pharaoh possibly look at this plague and still refuse to submit to the LORD? The Scriptures tell us that the LORD hardened the heart of Pharaoh.

This wording bothers a lot of preachers. They want to change it to say something else but I believe that the LORD said just what he meant. Let me see if I can help you see it. Pharaoh knew this was an action of the LORD. He saw Moses and Aaron throw the ashes into the air. Still he refused to acknowledge the LORD. He knew what the LORD wanted. Let my people go, that they may serve me. Still he refused to obey the LORD. The LORD has extended mercies toward Pharaoh multiple times and given him respite from the previous plagues. Yet Pharaoh still refuses to submit unto the LORD. Pharaoh has come to the point where even when he sees the hand of the LORD in his life, his self-righteousness, and pride has blinded him to the truth.

The Bible tells us there is a point where the LORD will let you be what you desire to be and He will harden your heart. I am going to read some verses that are not politically correct because they deal expressly with the sin of homosexuality but if we stubbornly refuse to hear the counsel of the LORD, we can suffer the same judgment for other sins.

Romans 1:21-24a, 26a, 28a

Because that, when they knew God, they glorified him not as God, neither were thankful; but became vain in their imaginations, and their foolish heart was darkened. [1:22] Professing themselves to be wise, they became fools, [1:23] And changed the glory of the uncorruptible God into an image made like to corruptible man, and to birds, and fourfooted beasts, and creeping things. [1:24] Wherefore God also gave them up ...

Romans 1:26

For this cause God gave them up ...

Romans 1:28

And even as they did not like to retain God in their knowledge, God gave them over to a reprobate mind...

What a terrible fate awaits those who harden their hearts against the LORD. They, too, can come to a place where the LORD will harden their hearts or give them up to their vain imaginations.

IV. Gods of Health

As with the other plagues, this plague strikes at the gods of the Egyptians. One of the few gods of the Egyptians that was actually a person was the god Imhotep (Figure 13). It is said that Imhotep was a very educated person that served a Pharaoh of the third dynasty (around 2700 BC). He was reported to be a priest, writer, a doctor, and a founder of the Egyptian studies of astronomy and architecture. Imhotep is associated with another god named Nefertem. This god was believed to help ease pain and suffering through medicine (Figure 14).

 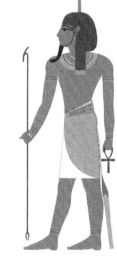

Figure 13   Figure 14

Yet, as with the other gods of Egypt, Nefertem or Imhotep could not stand before the LORD Jehovah. The LORD has struck against the Nile River, the life line of

Egypt. The Nile River's waters turned to blood, it brought forth a multitude of frogs and the Scriptures say that the land stank. The LORD struck against the soil of Egypt, the fertile fields brought forth plagues of lice and flies, instead of produce. The LORD struck against the wealth of Egypt, killing millions upon millions of cattle, camels, horses, and other livestock. With this plague, the LORD has struck against the physical health of the Egyptians.

Christians, I pray that your heart breaks for those that are hardening their hearts against the call of the LORD. It is easy for us to look and criticize but we are called to have compassion on those who are without Christ.

Jude 1:20-23

But ye, beloved, building up yourselves on your most holy faith, praying in the Holy Ghost, [1:21] Keep yourselves in the love of God, looking for the mercy of our Lord Jesus Christ unto eternal life. [1:22] And of some have compassion, making a difference: [1:23] And others save with fear, pulling them out of the fire; hating even the garment spotted by the flesh.

Pray that the LORD will use you to make a difference in the lives of those that He has placed within your circle of influence.

QUESTIONS

1. How should you live knowing that the LORD is not obligated to send us a specific warning of judgment?

2. Why do you think the LORD chose to use ashes from the ovens as a source of judgment rather than ashes from an altar?

3. Does knowing the people suffered for their leaders choices cause you any concern?

4. How do we pray for people's health and for the will of God at the same time?

5. How will you ensure that health will not become an idol in your life?

THE SEVENTH PLAGUE

Exodus 9:13-17

   And the LORD said unto Moses, Rise up early
in the morning, and stand before Pharaoh, and say
unto him, Thus saith the LORD God of the Hebrews,
Let my people go, that they may serve me. [9:14] For
I will at this time send all my plagues upon thine
heart, and upon thy servants, and upon thy people;
that thou mayest know that there is none like me in
all the earth. [9:15] For now I will stretch out my
hand, that I may smite thee and thy people with
pestilence; and thou shalt be cut off from the earth.
[9:16] And in very deed for this cause have I raised

123

thee up, for to shew in thee my power; and that my name may be declared throughout all the earth. [9:17] As yet exaltest thou thyself against my people, that thou wilt not let them go?

I. The LORD Sends

A. The Same Message

As in previous plagues, we read that the LORD is sending Moses and Aaron to stand before Pharaoh and deliver the message that has been delivered six times before. But there is a subtle change in the message that is delivered with this plague versus the message that has been delivered previously.

Thus saith the LORD God of the Hebrews, Let my people go, that they may serve me. Did you notice the change? The LORD has added the phrase "God of the Hebrews." I believe this phrase is added to make it clear that the reason there is a difference between the people of Israel and the people of Egypt is not just coincidence. The people of Israel serve the one, true, living God and there is no God beside Him. His name is the LORD Jehovah. He is the all-powerful, eternal, self-existent, holy, sin-hating, and covenant keeping God.

The LORD sends Moses and Aaron to make his demands known to Pharaoh again. Pharaoh can try to hide from the LORD but the LORD God of the Hebrews will not be ignored.

B. A Dire Warning

The sixth plague came without warning. It is the LORD's prerogative as to whether or not a warning is issued. Right on the heels of judgment without warning, the LORD extends mercy to Pharaoh. But this warning is given directly to Pharaoh. The plagues that are coming will affect the Egyptians but notice the direct appeal made toward Pharaoh.

Pharaoh has been marked for destruction. His stubborn refusals to receive the message and his persistence in hardening his heart against the demands of the LORD have brought him to a place that can only lead to death.

The LORD will send all His plagues against Pharaoh's heart. The physical plagues are terrifying. The physical plagues are troublesome. What will Pharaoh do when all the plagues of the LORD come upon his heart? When the LORD plagues his heart, Pharaoh will know that there is no other god like the LORD God of the Hebrews. Blow by blow and strike after strike the LORD will deliver plague upon plague upon Pharaoh's heart. Pharaoh will find no rest, no peace, or no hope as long as he refuses to obey the LORD.

The LORD says that Pharaoh shall be cut off from the earth. Pharaoh is marked for death. There is no other alternative for someone who refuses to hear, acknowledge, and obey the LORD.

Verse 16 reveals something else that is quite shocking for Pharaoh to hear. The LORD tells Pharaoh that he is not a ruler because of the gods of Egypt. He is not a ruler because he was born to the family of pharaohs. The LORD has brought this pagan king to the throne so that the power of the LORD may be revealed throughout all the earth. The passage ends with a warning to Pharaoh that can be restated as don't think more highly of yourself than you ought.

II. The Plague Described

Exodus 9:18-21

Behold, to morrow about this time I will cause it to rain a very grievous hail, such as hath not been in Egypt since the foundation thereof even until now. [9:19] Send therefore now, and gather thy cattle, and all that thou hast in the field; for upon every man and beast which shall be found in the field, and shall not be brought home, the hail shall come down upon them, and they shall die. [9:20] He that feared the word of the LORD among the servants of Pharaoh made his servants and his cattle flee into the houses: [9:21] And he that regarded not the word of the LORD left his servants and his cattle in the field.

A. Mercy Extended

We are given a brief description of the plague that is about to come upon Egypt. Before we look at the plague, I want to draw your attention to the mercy that is still being extended to Pharaoh and his people. The plague is not going to come upon them immediately. Behold, tomorrow the LORD says the plague will come. The LORD has once again given Pharaoh a choice and a chance.

The LORD is merciful. He is not willing that the unrighteous die.

Ezekiel 33:11

Say unto them, As I live, saith the Lord GOD, I have no pleasure in the death of the wicked; but that the wicked turn from his way and live: turn ye, turn ye from your evil ways; for why will ye die, O house of Israel?

The LORD has given Pharaoh a choice to make and He has given Pharaoh a chance to make it. He has the day and the night to consider what he will do with this information.

B. Some Believed

Notice that some of the Egyptians have decided that the LORD is the one true God. The servants of Pharaoh that feared the word of the LORD made preparations for their cattle and their servants. You may think that the plagues have been cruel and unusual punishment but the plagues were brought upon Pharaoh and the Egyptians so that they would know the LORD. Here we find that truly there are some Egyptians that have decided to forsake their false gods and obey the commands and observe the warnings of the LORD.

The LORD does not force anyone to follow Him. It is a personal decision. He that regardeth not the LORD left his servants and his property in the field. It is their choice.

III. The Plague Comes

Exodus 9:22-26

And the LORD said unto Moses, Stretch forth thine hand toward heaven, that there may be hail in all the land of Egypt, upon man, and upon beast, and upon every herb of the field, throughout the land of Egypt. [9:23] And Moses stretched forth his rod toward heaven: and the LORD sent thunder and hail, and the fire ran along upon the ground; and the LORD rained hail upon the land of Egypt. [9:24] So there was hail, and fire mingled with the hail, very grievous, such as there was none like it in all the land of Egypt since it became a nation. [9:25] And the hail smote throughout all the land of Egypt all that was in the field, both man and beast; and the hail smote every herb of the field, and brake every tree of the field. [9:26] Only in the land of Goshen, where the children of Israel were, was there no hail.

A. A Grievous Hail

The seventh plague is a plague of grievous hail. I did a little bit of research on hail stones and according to the National Weather Service the largest hail stone ever measured in the United States is about eight inches across, about twenty inches in diameter and weighed about two pounds. They say it was probably bigger but melted some before it could be measured and weighed. Unofficially a hailstone weighing over four pounds was said to have fallen in Kazakhstan in 1959.

A single hailstorm killed 246 people in India on April 30, 1888. More recently, 92 people were killed in Bangladesh by an April, 1986 hailstorm. One of the hail stones from the 1986 storm weighed over two pounds. (http://www.weather.com/outlook/weather-news/news/articles/hailstone-may-set-record_2010-07-27?page=2)

The Scriptures tell us that no hail storm like the one that was coming upon Egypt had ever been seen before. The hail was accompanied by thunder and the Scriptures say that fire ran along the ground.

Now some think the fire along the ground was lightning but the Hebrew word is not lightning, it means a burning, fiery, flaming hot fire. It could be lightning but if it was, it was a lightning that had never been seen before. So there are giant hail stones falling from the sky and there is a fire running along the ground at the same time.

B. The Destruction

The hail fell from the sky, the fire ran along the ground and this happened throughout all the land of Egypt. It smote all that were in the field, both man and beast. It also smote the crops. The herb of the field and the trees were broke. We are talking about a severe storm that destroys mammal and vegetable.

Think how frightening that must have been. If you have ever been through a really severe lightning storm you have some idea of how terrifying they can be. In 1991, my wife was home alone in such a storm. In a matter of less than two hours, nearly twelve inches of rain fell. The lightning accompanying this storm was almost constant. It made the night look like day. The power was out, roads were washed out, and homes were destroyed. Fortunately, no lives were lost. During this storm, I was fifty miles away and it didn't rain a drop.

While the Egyptians were going through this most terrifying of storms, the Israelites in the land of Goshen were safe. The LORD had established that the storm was only going to affect Pharaoh and those who had refused to obey His word.

IV. Pharaoh's Reaction

Exodus 9:27-35

And Pharaoh sent, and called for Moses and Aaron, and said unto them, I have sinned this time: the LORD is righteous, and I and my people are wicked. [9:28] Intreat the LORD (for it is enough) that there be no more mighty thunderings and hail; and I will let you go, and ye shall stay no longer. [9:29] And Moses said unto him, As soon as I am gone out of the city, I will spread abroad my hands unto the LORD; and the thunder shall cease, neither shall there be any more hail; that thou mayest know how that the earth is the LORD'S. [9:30] But as for thee and thy servants, I know that ye will not yet fear the LORD God. [9:31] And the flax and the barley was smitten: for the barley was in the ear, and the flax was bolled. [9:32] But the wheat and the rie were not smitten: for they were not grown up. [9:33] And Moses went out of the city from Pharaoh, and spread abroad his hands unto the LORD: and the thunders and hail ceased, and the rain was not poured upon the earth. [9:34] And when Pharaoh saw that the rain and the hail and the thunders were ceased, he sinned yet more, and hardened his heart, he and his servants. [9:35] And the heart of Pharaoh was hardened, neither would he let the children of Israel go; as the LORD had spoken by Moses.

A. Pharaoh's Request

Pharaoh sends someone to get Moses and Aaron and they appear before him. It would seem that the thunderings and the hail may still be going on at the time. Pharaoh has them brought to him and he says, I have sinned (this time). That's kind of a funny thing to say. He has sinned all the times before, too, but this plague seems to be a special case for him. He admits to his sin.

Pharaoh admits that the LORD is righteous and that he and his people are wicked. He then asks Moses to intreat the LORD for him. Please make this plague cease. It is enough. I see the LORD is God and I will let you go.

B. Moses' Response

Moses says, I will intreat the LORD for you and you will know that the LORD has heard because when I leave the city, I will lift up my arms and the storm will cease. But Moses is no fool. He speaks rather plainly with Pharaoh. He says I know that you do not fear the LORD, yet.

Tragedy can bring people to say and do things they would not normally say or do. This plague has brought Pharaoh to a place where he will say anything to get the plague to end but he has no intention of surrendering his will to the LORD.

Looking to verses 31 and 32, we can know the time of the year for this plague. The first message of Moses was delivered after the early harvest of the year. Most commentators believe this makes sense for that would be when the Israelites could easily gather stubble to make bricks. This would equate to about our months of April or May. The actual plagues are thought to have begun toward the end of June, and continued at various intervals until this plague which coincides with our month of February.

When Moses leaves the city, he lifts up his hands toward the heavens and the hail, thunder, and fire stops. Pharaoh hardens his heart and will not let the people go. The crisis is over and he returns to being the same Pharaoh he was before the hail and thunder and fire fell.

V. Gods and Goddesses of Weather

This plague brings destruction and even death to men, animals, and crops of Egypt. The Egyptians worshipped gods of weather like Tefnut, the goddess of moisture (Figure 15) and Set, the god of weather who had a voice of thunder (Figure 16). The Egyptians also worshipped a god named Ami, who was the god of fire and Maahes, the god of storms. But the LORD God of the Hebrews is the only true and living God.

Figure 15   Figure 16

This plague has moved beyond the Nile River and the land of Egypt to show that the LORD is also ruler over the weather of Egypt, too. No matter which god or goddess Pharaoh would turn to hoping to find a reprieve, he finds they are no match for Jehovah.

QUESTIONS

1. How did you feel reading the LORD Himself would smite Pharaoh?

2. How should we live knowing the LORD God of the Hebrews is the LORD of all the earth?

3. Has there been a negative experience that has brought you to or closer to the LORD?

4. How can we ensure that we are seeking the LORD and not just an end to our current troubles?

5. Is it comforting to know that the LORD is in control and uses all things to display His power and glory?

THE EIGHTH PLAGUE

Exodus 10:1-3

And the LORD said unto Moses, Go in unto Pharaoh: for I have hardened his heart, and the heart of his servants, that I might shew these my signs before him: [10:2] And that thou mayest tell in the ears of thy son, and of thy son's son, what things I have wrought in Egypt, and my signs which I have done among them; that ye may know how that I am the LORD. [10:3] And Moses and Aaron came in unto Pharaoh, and said unto him, Thus saith the LORD God of the Hebrews, How long wilt thou

139

refuse to humble thyself before me? let my people go, that they may serve me.

I. The Message

A. The LORD Explains

Now, if I am Moses and Aaron, I am going to start to struggle with this constant going before Pharaoh and his constant lying to me. I am going to struggle with his constant hardening of his heart. We have seen Moses chide Pharaoh for his refusals and his lying. Moses and Aaron would probably struggle with the sight of the destruction and the suffering of the Egyptian people. In this passage, we see the LORD giving Moses and Aaron a little pep talk. The LORD does not have to explain Himself to you but sometimes He will.

Maybe during their prayer time, Moses and Aaron have started comparing notes and they have said what's the use or what is the purpose of what we are doing. It does not seem to be doing any good. That's when the LORD steps in and reminds them that it is the LORD that is in control. The LORD has hardened the heart of Pharaoh so that that He might shew forth His mighty signs.

The LORD says, Pharaoh is not going to listen but I will still deliver you. Someday all these events will be told to your children and their children and their children's children. We are thousands of years removed from the events that we are reading and yet we are still telling our children of the mighty works of God. The result of the telling of the mighty works of LORD is that they will know that I am the LORD.

Are you discouraged? Does it seem that when you give the message of the LORD the people's hearts are hard? Do you want to give up and shrug your shoulders and ask, what is the use? The LORD says these things are happening under His control and with the purpose that you and your children can know that He is the self-existent, holy, sin-hating, eternal, and covenant keeping God. Now hold your head up and get back out there and deliver His message!

B. The Message

In this message, we see the LORD reproves Pharaoh. How long will you refuse to humble yourself before Me? Pharaoh is the great Pharaoh. He is the ruler of Egypt. He is portrayed as a god. Yet the true and living God demands that even the greatest of men upon the earth humble themselves before Him.

The Bible is replete with examples of men that have refused to humble themselves before the LORD. However, those that have refused to humble themselves have eventually been brought low. In Daniel 4, we have recorded the pride of Nebuchadnezzar. Is this not great Babylon that I have built by might and by my power and for my glory? And while the words were still in his mouth the LORD said thy kingdom is departed from thee. In the next verses, we read that the mighty king is eating grass in the field like an ox and is out of his mind. But when the king repents he says these words:

Daniel 4:37

Now I Nebuchadnezzar praise and extol and honour the King of heaven, all whose works are truth, and his ways judgment: and those that walk in pride he is able to abase.

The message is the same as the very first time Moses and Aaron spoke with Pharaoh. Let my people go that they may serve me. It is a simple message. The LORD is calling His people to be set free from bondage that they may serve Him. The message is a demonstration of God's victorious power over the kingdom of Satan. He has set his people free from Pharaoh and He is able to set us free from the bondage and burden of sin!

II. The Plague

Exodus 10:4-15

Else, if thou refuse to let my people go, behold, to morrow will I bring the locusts into thy coast: [10:5] And they shall cover the face of the earth, that one cannot be able to see the earth: and they shall eat the residue of that which is escaped, which remaineth unto you from the hail, and shall eat every tree which groweth for you out of the field: [10:6] And they shall fill thy houses, and the houses of all thy servants, and the houses of all the Egyptians; which neither thy fathers, nor thy fathers' fathers have seen, since the day that they were upon the earth unto this day. And he turned himself, and went out from Pharaoh.

A. The Announcement

Moses comes and stands before Pharaoh. He tells Pharaoh that if he does not let the people go that they may worship the LORD, then a plague of locust will come upon the land. The locusts will cover the ground. The locust will eat the wheat and the rye that were not destroyed by the hail. They would strip the green off the trees that were not destroyed by the hail. They will be in your house, in your servant's houses, and in the houses of all your people. This plague, a swarm of locusts, will be worse than anything your fathers have ever seen.

I like it that Moses simply turns around and walks out. There is still mercy in this plague. The LORD is giving Pharaoh a chance. The plague is not going to come until tomorrow. I believe that this was done to give Pharaoh some time to consider what he would do. He is given a chance and he has to make a choice. For the first time Pharaoh's advisors speak up.

B. The Compromise

Exodus 10:7-11

And Pharaoh's servants said unto him, How long shall this man be a snare unto us? let the men go, that they may serve the LORD their God: knowest thou not yet that Egypt is destroyed? [10:8] And Moses and Aaron were brought again unto Pharaoh: and he said unto them, Go, serve the LORD your God: but who are they that shall go? [10:9] And Moses said, We will go with our young and with our

143

old, with our sons and with our daughters, with our flocks and with our herds will we go; for we must hold a feast unto the LORD. [10:10] And he said unto them, Let the LORD be so with you, as I will let you go, and your little ones: look to it; for evil is before you. [10:11] Not so: go now ye that are men, and serve the LORD; for that ye did desire. And they were driven out from Pharaoh's presence.

Pharaoh's servants ask Pharaoh, how long are you going to let these guys bring trouble upon our people? The advisors have not accepted the LORD as their God but they have seen enough. Look around you, Egypt is destroyed. Let the men go that they may serve the LORD their God.

I suppose that Pharaoh sent messengers to bring Moses and Aaron back and when they came back in Pharaoh speaks to them. He tells them that the Hebrews can go and they can serve the LORD but he asks who is it that shall go. The compromise is that they will let the males go but they will not let the women and children go.

Moses answers and says that we are taking everyone. We are taking the old and the young, the boys and the girls, and all of our flocks and herds. Every one of the Hebrews is going to hold this feast unto the LORD.

Pharaoh rejects this out of hand. In effect he says, over my dead body! I will allow you to go and serve the LORD but only those that are males. You must leave your wives and your children and your possessions here. Pharaoh then drives Moses and Aaron out of his presence.

This is what Satan tries to do to us even today. The LORD is calling you to serve Him. He wants you to serve Him with all of your possessions and all of your being. We call it being sold out for God. I surrender all I have and all that I am to Him and then I serve Him. Satan tries to get us to compromise. Serve the LORD, he says, but don't tithe. Serve the LORD but don't be a fanatic. Serve the LORD but don't give up the sins that are besetting us! This is unacceptable to the LORD.

C. The Locusts

Exodus 10:12-15

And the LORD said unto Moses, Stretch out thine hand over the land of Egypt for the locusts, that they may come up upon the land of Egypt, and eat every herb of the land, even all that the hail hath left. [10:13] And Moses stretched forth his rod over the land of Egypt, and the LORD brought an east wind upon the land all that day, and all that night; and when it was morning, the east wind brought the locusts. [10:14] And the locusts went up over all the land of Egypt, and rested in all the coasts of Egypt: very grievous were they; before them there were no such locusts as they, neither after them shall be such. [10:15] For they covered the face of the whole earth, so that the land was darkened; and they did eat every herb of the land, and all the fruit of the trees which the hail had left: and there remained not any green thing in the trees, or in the herbs of the field, through all the land of Egypt.

As Moses and Aaron depart from Pharaoh, Moses lifts up the rod and an east wind begins to blow. That east wind blew all that day and all that night and in the morning that east wind brought the locusts into the land of Egypt.

The locusts cover the ground. The locusts ate everything that was green that had not been destroyed by the hail. This plague was described as grievous and the likes of it had never been seen before.

Locust swarms are common in Egypt and I found several sites documenting locust swarms. There are breeding areas in Saudi Arabia and when conditions are right (a strong wind) the swarms can cross the Red Sea in search for food. Locusts can travel up to six-hundred miles in as little as twenty-four hours. Locusts are particularly fond of eating tender plants.

I read about a swarm of locusts that invaded Egypt in 2004. According to the Minister of Agriculture, the swarm was forty-four miles in length and contained several hundred million locusts. He said this swarm was reminiscent of the Biblical plague.

Locusts are very destructive because of their voracious appetites. A locust can eat about a tenth of an ounce of food (its own body weight) each day. That does not sound like a very big deal but pound for pound a locust eats 60 to 100 times as much as a human being. Each square mile of locusts is estimated to eat up to 720 tons of food every day. That would be enough food to feed 200,000 humans. So this terrible plague comes upon

Egypt and the locusts are everywhere and eating everything.

III. Pharaoh's Reaction

Exodus 10:16-20

Then Pharaoh called for Moses and Aaron in haste; and he said, I have sinned against the LORD your God, and against you. [10:17] Now therefore forgive, I pray thee, my sin only this once, and intreat the LORD your God, that he may take away from me this death only. [10:18] And he went out from Pharaoh, and intreated the LORD. [10:19] And the LORD turned a mighty strong west wind, which took away the locusts, and cast them into the Red sea; there remained not one locust in all the coasts of Egypt. [10:20] But the LORD hardened Pharaoh's heart, so that he would not let the children of Israel go.

A. Called in Haste

It is interesting to note that Pharaoh had driven Moses and Aaron out of his presence but now he is sending for them in haste. He must have them come and he must have this plague stopped quickly. Egypt is already destroyed. The cattle are dead, the people have been afflicted, the crops destroyed, and now what is left is being devoured by the locusts. He was full of pride when he drove them out but now he implores them to return and to return quickly.

Pharaoh also calls this plague death. This plague has his full attention. He asks Moses to forgive him, pray for him, and take away this death. He makes no promises to let them go but he simply pleads for this plague to be removed.

B. Moses Prays

Moses leaves the presence of Pharaoh and he prays to the LORD and the LORD removes this plague. The East winds brought the plague and the West winds removed them. Even the winds obey the LORD. The locusts are removed from the land.

C. Pharaoh's Heart

Once again the LORD hardens Pharaoh's heart. It does not make any sense that Pharaoh could look at the miracles of the LORD and still refuse to humble himself before the LORD. He knows the plagues are the work of the LORD. He knows the plagues are coming upon his heart. Pharaoh knows it is the LORD that is removing each plague. Still he has rejected the LORD. At this point, the actions of the LORD only harden his heart.

IV. Agricultural gods

Egypt had several gods and goddesses of agriculture that they believed protected the growing of the crops and the harvesting of the crops. Osiris and Isis (Figure 17) are two examples of these gods and goddesses.

Figure 17

Osiris' green skin symbolized the fertile soil needed to grow crops. It was believed that Osiris provided these vital nutrients to the land of Egypt through the annual flooding of the Nile River. He is included in Figure 4 (page 47) as one of the Nile River gods and is depicted with wheat growing out of his bier.

149

Isis is the sister wife of Osiris. She is credited with teaching women skills necessary to be a good wife including growing crops, grinding corn, and making bread. As in the other plagues, these gods and goddesses could not stand before the one true living God, the LORD God of the Hebrews.

QUESTIONS

1. How do you respond to the suffering of others?

2. Has there been a time when your pride has kept you from admitting you were wrong?

3. Does it surprise you that the LORD is still willing to give Pharaoh a chance to repent before this plague comes?

4. How can you ensure that your worship of the LORD includes all members of your family?

5. Would you be willing to come quickly and pray for someone who has mistreated you?

THE NINTH PLAGUE

Exodus 10:21-29

And the LORD said unto Moses, Stretch out thine hand toward heaven, that there may be darkness over the land of Egypt, even darkness which may be felt. [10:22] And Moses stretched forth his hand toward heaven; and there was a thick darkness in all the land of Egypt three days: [10:23] They saw not one another, neither rose any from his place for three days: but all the children of Israel had light in their dwellings. [10:24] And Pharaoh called unto Moses, and said, Go ye, serve the LORD; only let your flocks and your herds be stayed: let your little ones also go with you. [10:25] And Moses said, Thou

must give us also sacrifices and burnt offerings, that
we may sacrifice unto the LORD our God. [10:26]
Our cattle also shall go with us; there shall not an
hoof be left behind; for thereof must we take to serve
the LORD our God; and we know not with what we
must serve the LORD, until we come thither. [10:27]
But the LORD hardened Pharaoh's heart, and he
would not let them go. [10:28] And Pharaoh said unto
him, Get thee from me, take heed to thyself, see my
face no more; for in that day thou seest my face thou
shalt die. [10:29] And Moses said, Thou hast spoken
well, I will see thy face again no more.

I. The Plague Comes

A. Without Warning

As we look to the ninth plague, I will remind you
that every third plague has been brought without any
warning from the LORD. The LORD is merciful. The
LORD is long suffering. The LORD is not willing that any
should perish but that all may come to know Him. But do
not presume upon the goodness, graciousness, and mercy
of the LORD. He is not required nor is He obligated to
give us warning before judgment comes upon us.

Pharaoh knows what the LORD desires and if
Pharaoh refuses to obey, he will be judged. The same is
true for any of us in this day. If the LORD has sent His
messengers and His message to you and you have
stubbornly refused to obey Him, He may send a plague
upon you without warning.

B. The Plague Described

The plague is a plague of darkness. Darkness is often terrifying for children. I even know of a young lady that, even though she is married and expecting a child of her own, she is afraid of the dark. There is just something about not being able to see what is around us that is troubling to us. This plague is not just any darkness. Did you notice how it is described? It is a darkness that can be felt.

Scholars seem to be divided over the exact cause of the darkness. Some think it was a thick fog or heavy mist that blotted out the sun and made it impossible to kindle a flame. I suppose they would say it is something akin to our saying, thicker than pea soup.

That is one possible explanation but it is more likely that the darkness was caused by what is called chamsin. What is a chamsin? It is a dry, hot and dusty southwesterly wind blowing across the Sahara Desert that carries massive amounts of sand into Egypt. The winds of the chamsin can reach over ninety mph and can cause temperatures to rise over forty degrees Fahrenheit in just a couple of hours.

I would remind you that the locust came in by a steady East wind and they were removed by a westerly wind. That wind was so strong that there was not left a single locust in all the land of Egypt. So it is quite possible that the wind that blew the locusts out of Egypt intensified and created this plague of darkness.

155

The effect of the wind makes it impossible to do anything. There are recorded accounts of Napoleon's forces facing a chamsin. They said the distant sky turned a strange color. Anyone that did not take shelter before the storm reached them found it to be a suffocating wall of dust, choking and blinding them. This would be a darkness that could be felt.

C. The Plague's Extent

Moses lifts his hands toward the heaven and the darkness comes upon the land of Egypt. It is described as a thick darkness and it lasted for three days. For three days, this west wind blows blotting out the sun, bringing in the sand and keeping temperatures hot. This storm was so bad that the Egyptians did not see one another and they did not go anywhere for three days.

Imagine being an Egyptian and not being able to see anything because of the darkness. Imagine hearing this wind blowing against your home. Imagine how terrifying this would be if it lasted for an hour, what about four hours, what about twenty-four hours? This storm and this darkness lasted for three days.

If the storm itself would not be terrifying enough, some Jewish traditions teach that the LORD also sent evil angels to plague the people in their darkness. You may say, I don't think the LORD would do that, well take it up with the LORD. In one of the Psalms, written about the plagues upon Egypt, we read these words:

Psalms 78:49

He cast upon them the fierceness of his anger, wrath, and indignation, and trouble, by sending evil angels among them.

D. The Distinction

Notice that all the children of Israel had light in their dwellings. All of them had light. This was a time of despair, fear, and desperation for the Egyptians but for the Israelites it was not. The Hebrews were not suffering as those who would not submit to the call of the LORD.

The LORD is showing His mercy! In the eyes of the Egyptians, the Israelites were just slaves; they were just property to be used and abused. But in the eyes of the LORD the Israelites were His chosen people. They are His chosen people. They will bring a blessing unto all the people of the earth.

The LORD may not always exclude His people from going through trouble but be sure of this, He can! The Israelites have come to see that the LORD is God and Jehovah is His name. They are willing to submit and obey. They do not need to be judged or corrected and here we see the LORD spares them from the sufferings of the unrighteous.

E. Pharaoh Reacts

We are not told what Pharaoh or his advisors do during the three days. We must suppose that they, like all the other Egyptians, don't stir. They are expecting this chamsin to subside as they normally do after only an hour or two; however, after three days, Pharaoh knows that this is the hand of the LORD striking against his heart with another plague.

After three days, Pharaoh finally gathers his advisors and says, what do you suppose is going on and what do you think we should do about it? In my imagination, I can see the room fall silent as one of the magicians clears his throat and says, I believe this has probably been another plague from the LORD God of the Hebrews and you should probably send someone to get Moses and Aaron, sir. Whether that happened or not, I do not know but Pharaoh does send for Moses and Aaron and he tells them go and serve the LORD.

Once again, Pharaoh tries to put a stipulation on serving the LORD. He says, you can take the men and women, young and old but you must leave your flocks here. Pharaoh is trying to maintain a hold over the Hebrews. He wants to ensure that the people will not make a complete break from Egypt. He needs something to keep them tied to the land of their bondage.

Moses refuses the compromise. He says, not so. We must take all of the herds and flocks because we do not know how many or what type of sacrifices that the LORD will require of us. We will not leave one hoof behind.

Praise the LORD! That is being fully committed to serving the LORD. I will go where you want me to go and I will do what you want me to do. I will surrender my all to Jesus! I love the answer that Moses gave to Pharaoh but Pharaoh does not.

Pharaoh knew Moses and Aaron would not consent to a compromise but he still refuses to submit to the will of the LORD. These words are so sad; the LORD hardens Pharaoh's heart. Pharaoh refuses and says I will not let you go and this time he adds, if you see my face again, I will kill you.

II. God of the Sun

Perhaps the most powerful god in all of Egyptian mythology is Amen-Ra, the sun god (Figure 18). Amen-Ra represented light, warmth, and growth but for three days the LORD had rendered Amen-Ra to be powerless. There was no light, no warmth, and no growth. Once again, the LORD has demonstrated that He alone is the one true living God.

Figure 18

QUESTIONS

1. Do you think that God should declare specific warnings before a plague comes?

2. What do you think of the LORD using the same wind that removed locusts to bring the plague of darkness?

3. How would you equate the physical darkness of the plague to the spiritual darkness of sin?

4. How would you equate the physical light of the Hebrews to the spiritual light of the Gospel?

5. Are you willing to fully commit to serving the LORD, no matter the consequences?

THE TENTH PLAGUE

Exodus 11:1-10, 12:29-37

Exodus 11:1-3

And the LORD said unto Moses, Yet will I bring one plague more upon Pharaoh, and upon Egypt; afterwards he will let you go hence: when he shall let you go, he shall surely thrust you out hence altogether. [11:2] Speak now in the ears of the people, and let every man borrow of his neighbour, and every woman of her neighbour, jewels of silver, and jewels of gold. [11:3] And the LORD gave the people favour in the sight of the Egyptians. Moreover the man Moses was very great in the land of Egypt, in the

163

sight of Pharaoh's servants, and in the sight of the people.

I. The LORD's Message to Moses

A. The Assurance of the LORD

At the conclusion of chapter number ten of Exodus, Moses was standing before Pharaoh. Pharaoh enraged by the plagues has told Moses that the next time he sees Pharaoh's face he shall die. At the beginning of chapter eleven, Moses has not yet left the presence of Pharaoh. Before Moses leaves, the LORD has him give one last warning to Pharaoh about the final plague.

Notice the assurance that the LORD gives to Moses. We have often been told that if the LORD says something once you can believe it. If He says something twice, you had better pay attention. In this passage, the LORD says three times that Pharaoh is going to let them go.

The LORD says, he will let you go, he shall let you go, and he shall surely thrust you out. Now these phrases are positive but notice their intensification. He will let you go, that sounds like asking dad for something and he says yeah, go ahead. It is like he does not really care. The second phrase is he shall let you go and this is more emphatic. The LORD says it is certain, Pharaoh will let you go. The third phrase says not only will Pharaoh let you go but he certainly will insist and drive you out of the land.

You may not be able to see the end of the trial or circumstance that you find yourself in today but let me tell you that the LORD can see it. He gives us assurance. I was reading the 23rd Psalm and I found it to be full of the comfort and assurance of the LORD.

Psalms 23:1-6

The LORD is my shepherd; I shall not want. [23:2] He maketh me to lie down in green pastures: he leadeth me beside the still waters. [23:3] He restoreth my soul: he leadeth me in the paths of righteousness for his name's sake. [23:4] Yea, though I walk through the valley of the shadow of death, I will fear no evil: for thou art with me; thy rod and thy staff they comfort me. [23:5] Thou preparest a table before me in the presence of mine enemies: thou anointest my head with oil; my cup runneth over. [23:6] Surely goodness and mercy shall follow me all the days of my life: and I will dwell in the house of the LORD for ever.

Think on these phrases of promise and comfort; He maketh me to lie down in green pastures, He leadeth me beside still waters, He restoreth my soul, He leadeth me in the paths of righteousness, and thou art with me. Moses is in a tough situation but the LORD has given him assurance and we can trust in the LORD, too!

B. The Blessings of the LORD

We see that the LORD is going to bless the Hebrews. He says to them, go and borrow from the Egyptians. The Egyptians were their masters and had abused them and profited from them. The LORD is about to bless the Hebrews at the hands of their masters. They borrow jewels of silver and jewels of gold. Most astounding is that the Egyptians are willing to give to the Hebrews.

Moses, an abandoned child of a slave, a reject to society, and a fugitive has become great in the eyes of the people of Egypt. He speaks the words of the LORD and when he prays, the LORD hears and answers him. When the Hebrews go and say to their neighbors that Moses has sent us to ask of you jewels of silver and jewels of gold, the Egyptians give them to the Hebrews. You see the LORD is about to deliver the Hebrews out of bondage and He is not going to deliver them empty handed.

II. The LORD's Message to Pharaoh

Exodus 11:4-10

And Moses said, Thus saith the LORD, About midnight will I go out into the midst of Egypt: [11:5] And all the firstborn in the land of Egypt shall die, from the firstborn of Pharaoh that sitteth upon his throne, even unto the firstborn of the maidservant that is behind the mill; and all the firstborn of beasts. [11:6] And there shall be a great cry throughout all the land of Egypt, such as there was none like it, nor shall be like it any more. [11:7] But against any of the children of Israel shall not a dog move his tongue, against man or beast: that ye may know how that the LORD doth put a difference between the Egyptians and Israel. [11:8] And all these thy servants shall come down unto me, and bow down themselves unto me, saying, Get thee out, and all the people that follow thee: and after that I will go out. And he went out from Pharaoh in a great anger. [11:9] And the LORD said unto Moses, Pharaoh shall not hearken unto you; that my wonders may be multiplied in the land of Egypt. [11:10] And Moses and Aaron did all these wonders before Pharaoh: and the LORD hardened Pharaoh's heart, so that he would not let the children of Israel go out of his land.

A. The Warning

In this final plague, the LORD says that He will pass through the land of Egypt and He will slay the first born of all the sons of Egypt. Many have asked why the LORD would ever consider such a terrible plague. It is as if they think this plague came out of nowhere. If we look back to Exodus chapter four, we find that this plague, the last and most dreadful of them all, should not come as a surprise to Pharaoh.

Exodus 4:22-23

And thou shalt say unto Pharaoh, Thus saith the LORD, Israel is my son, even my firstborn: [4:23] And I say unto thee, Let my son go, that he may serve me: and if thou refuse to let him go, behold, I will slay thy son, even thy firstborn.

All the other plagues had come as a warning that a worse plague was on its way. The LORD has offered mercy and given Pharaoh chance after chance to make the right choice but Pharaoh has stubbornly refused until he must face this final terrible plague.

Even in this instance, there is a chance for Pharaoh to repent. The midnight is not the one immediately following the plague of darkness. There are at least four days or more that are necessary for the Hebrews to prepare for the Passover. So even in this judgment Pharaoh has time to reconsider and time to make the decision to obey the LORD.

This plague will touch all Egyptian people. Do not think that this will only be against the poor or against the evil in society. From the highest political power in the land to the lowliest slave, no one that rejects the LORD will be safe. This plague will not only be upon the people but it will be upon the beasts as well. The LORD is going to demonstrate His power over all life.

The result of this plague is that the land will be filled with a great cry. This is not a crying of tears but a great, loud, prolonged shrieking throughout the land of Egypt. The Egyptian people have suffered greatly under these plagues and the losses have been mounting. It is not until this final plague that the Egyptian people scream out in the pain of loss of their child and the pain of the loss of their livestock.

I believe that we have fallen into a mindset that says because the LORD's judgment is not immediate that we are safe from it. I believe that we tend to think that we are too good or too well off for the plagues that are affecting others to affect us. The plagues against Egypt are recorded to give us a warning! Do not presume upon the goodness and graciousness of the LORD. He is merciful and He wants all men and women and boys and girls to come to repentance but there will come a day when you will be judged. No matter how well respected you were in the community. No matter what you did on the school board or at the office or at the church, judgment day will come for all of us.

B. The Distinction

Once again, we find that the LORD makes a distinction between the Hebrews and the Egyptians. The phrase used here about not even a dog shall move his tongue represents that there will not even be any dogs fighting in the land of Goshen. On the night when Egypt shall be judged, there will be quietness and peace in the land of Goshen.

The difference is that the Hebrews know the LORD as Jehovah, the self-existent, holy, sin-hating, eternal, all powerful, and covenant keeping God. This distinction is so clear on this day of judgment that the Egyptians will come and beg Moses and the Hebrews to leave. Once Moses delivers this final warning, he turns and leaves from the presence of Pharaoh.

C. The Refusal

Once again we read these sad words, Pharaoh will not hearken unto you and the LORD hardened Pharaoh's heart. Pharaoh knows what the LORD requires. He knows what the LORD wants. He has heard the message and he has seen the LORD's power and yet he still refuses to accept that the LORD is God and Jehovah is his name. It would seem that with every overture of the LORD Pharaoh recoils in horror and disgust. His heart, hardened so many times before by his own stubborn will, now finds any mention of the LORD as repulsive. Pharaoh has come to a place where he is without hope and he is determined for destruction.

III. The Plague Comes

Exodus 12:29-37

And it came to pass, that at midnight the LORD smote all the firstborn in the land of Egypt, from the firstborn of Pharaoh that sat on his throne unto the firstborn of the captive that was in the dungeon; and all the firstborn of cattle. [12:30] And Pharaoh rose up in the night, he, and all his servants, and all the Egyptians; and there was a great cry in Egypt; for there was not a house where there was not one dead. [12:31] And he called for Moses and Aaron by night, and said, Rise up, and get you forth from among my people, both ye and the children of Israel; and go, serve the LORD, as ye have said. [12:32] Also take your flocks and your herds, as ye have said, and be gone; and bless me also. [12:33] And the Egyptians were urgent upon the people, that they might send them out of the land in haste; for they said, We be all dead men. [12:34] And the people took their dough before it was leavened, their kneadingtroughs being bound up in their clothes upon their shoulders. [12:35] And the children of Israel did according to the word of Moses; and they borrowed of the Egyptians jewels of silver, and jewels of gold, and raiment: [12:36] And the LORD gave the people favour in the sight of the Egyptians, so that they lent unto them such things as they required. And they spoiled the Egyptians. [12:37] And the children of Israel journeyed from Rameses to Succoth, about six hundred thousand on foot that were men, beside children.

A. The Firstborn Die

At least four days have passed since Moses stood before Pharaoh. No doubt the sun was shining, the birds singing, and gentle cool breezes blew over the land. Pharaoh and his servants have begun to wonder if maybe this time the LORD could not or would not fulfill His word. It is an ordinary day just like any other day before the plagues had ever come upon the land. As the days have passed since the last confrontation, the fear of the judgment of the LORD has waned.

The Scriptures say, and it came to pass, just as the LORD had spoken. The firstborn from Pharaoh's house to the house of the prisoner in the dungeon died. The firstborn of the livestock died. The land was filled with a loud, prolonged shrieking like nothing ever heard before. There was not a single home in Egypt that was not affected by this plague. There was not a single house where there was not one dead.

B. Pharaoh Reacts

Pharaoh had previously said I do not want to ever see you again but now he calls for Moses and Aaron to beg them or urge them to leave.

Pharaoh says, rise up, get thee forth, go, and be gone. In all the times before, he has refused to let them go but now he is commanding them to go and to do so immediately. There is no attempt to compromise. He says go, take all your people, men and women, boys and girls, old and young. Take your flocks and your herds as you have said and be gone.

The advisors to Pharaoh had said that they should let them go because Egypt is destroyed. Pharaoh, after the locusts, said remove this death from me and now as the Egyptians assess the situation they say the Hebrews must go or we will all be dead men.

C. The LORD Delivers

The Hebrews had prepared for this night and when they were urged to go, they left. Their bread was unleavened because their kneading troughs were packed up. The Hebrews borrowed the jewels of silver and gold from the Egyptians and the Egyptians gladly gave to them.

The Scriptures say that the Hebrews spoiled the Egyptians. It was as if the Hebrews had gone to war against the Egyptians and had defeated them. They carried off the wealth of the Egyptians and never fired a shot.

Six hundred thousand Hebrew men came out of Egypt. It is likely that more than three million Hebrews left Egypt that night. It is also worth noting that it was not just Hebrews that left Egypt that night. The Scriptures say a mixed multitude came out. I believe that even some of the Egyptians have decided that the LORD is God, Jehovah is His name, and we will be His people.

IV. God and Goddess of Children

A. Bes

Many of the gods and goddesses of Egypt had some connection to fertility but for this study we will consider just two of them. Bes is probably one of the most unusual of all of the Egyptian gods (Figure 19). His appearance is very much that of something other than an Egyptian. Adding to his uniqueness is that he is almost always depicted from a full front view rather than the normal profile view of most gods.

It was believed that during the birth of a child, Bes would dance about the room to protect the child from evil gods. He was also believed to stay nearby the child to entertain them. Egyptians attributed Bes as being the cause of the laughter or smile of a baby.

Figure 19

B. Meskhenet

Meskhenet was said to be the goddess of the birthing houses and acted as a divine midwife (Figure 20). Other attributes would include her ability to assign a person's destiny in this life and the next. She was thought to be a protector from birth to death and into the afterlife.

Figure 20

This final plague shows that indeed it is the LORD who is the one true living God. None of the gods or goddesses of Egypt could stand before Him.

QUESTIONS

1. What verses of Scriptures do you look to for comfort or assurance?

2. Why is the punishment of the death of the first born justified?

3. Does the fact that the LORD does not punish sin immediately make it easier to sin?

4. How will you keep your heart receptive to the correction of the LORD?

5. Has there been a time where the LORD not only delivered you but blessed you in the process?

THE PASSOVER

Exodus 12:1-27

Exodus 12:1-6

And the LORD spake unto Moses and Aaron in the land of Egypt, saying, [12:2] This month shall be unto you the beginning of months: it shall be the first month of the year to you. [12:3] Speak ye unto all the congregation of Israel, saying, In the tenth day of this month they shall take to them every man a lamb, according to the house of their fathers, a lamb for an house: [12:4] And if the household be too little for the lamb, let him and his neighbour next unto his house

*take it according to the number of the souls; every
man according to his eating shall make your count for
the lamb. [12:5] Your lamb shall be without blemish,
a male of the first year: ye shall take it out from the
sheep, or from the goats: [12:6] And ye shall keep it
up until the fourteenth day of the same month: and
the whole assembly of the congregation of Israel shall
kill it in the evening.*

I. Passover Established

A. Established by the LORD

The LORD spoke to Moses and it is the LORD
that has established the Passover. I think it is worth noting
that this is not a manmade celebration. The LORD
dictated every detail of the Passover. He starts by
establishing a new beginning of the year.

B. A New Beginning

Undoubtedly, the Hebrews followed the Egyptian
calendar, but no more. The LORD said this month shall
be unto you the beginning of months and it shall be the
first month of the year to you.

This would be most equal to our March or April.
The fluctuation is not due to uncertainty but due to the
fact that the Hebrews followed a lunar calendar and we do
not. Believe it or not, Easter, which is connected with the
Passover, does not move. You say, it does on my calendar.
Yes, it is true but it is always the same on the Hebrew
calendar that was ordained by the LORD.

On the tenth day of the month, every home was to set aside a lamb. If a home was not large enough to eat the entire lamb, they were to observe the Passover with their neighbor. Josephus, a great Jewish historian, says that there were seldom fewer than ten people to a lamb, and often as many as twenty people. The Jewish Rabbi's later wrote "they do not kill the Passover lamb for a single person, nor even for a society consisting of one hundred, that cannot eat the quantity of an olive." The LORD's Passover is established so that every man can be filled according to His eating.

So on the tenth day the lamb is set aside and it is then kept to the fourteenth day. On the evening of the fourteenth day, the lamb is slain. There have been many suppositions as to why the lambs were set aside for the four days. At least two Jewish rabbis taught that the lamb was to be a witness to the Egyptians. Perhaps an Egyptian walking past a Hebrew home would see the lamb and ask, "Why are you keeping this particular lamb?", and then the Hebrew could tell him of the judgment yet to come.

After the four days, the lamb is slain. The people did not come together in one place to slay the lambs but every home was to slay the lamb at exactly the same time.

II. Specific instructions

A. Concerning the Blood

Exodus 12:7

> *And they shall take of the blood, and strike it on the two side posts and on the upper door post of the houses, wherein they shall eat it.*

Exodus 12:13

> *And the blood shall be to you for a token upon the houses where ye are: and when I see the blood, I will pass over you, and the plague shall not be upon you to destroy you, when I smite the land of Egypt.*

Exodus 12:21-22

> *Then Moses called for all the elders of Israel, and said unto them, Draw out and take you a lamb according to your families, and kill the passover. [12:22] And ye shall take a bunch of hyssop, and dip it in the blood that is in the bason, and strike the lintel and the two side posts with the blood that is in the bason; and none of you shall go out at the door of his house until the morning.*

The LORD told Moses to tell the people they were to catch the blood in a bason, a bowl, and they were to take some hyssop, a plant that commonly grew in the area, and dip it in the blood and then strike the hyssop upon the door posts. They are not to sprinkle the blood of the lamb on the door posts but they are to apply it, on purpose, to the door posts.

The blood was to be a sign. When the LORD passed through Egypt that night, He would see the blood and pass over that home.

The two posts with the lintel represented the door, which they surrounded; and the doorway through which the house was entered stood for the house itself. There was only a portion of the doorway that was not to have blood applied to it and that was the threshold. The blood of the lamb is not something to trifle with and it is not to be trodden under foot.

The blood was a form of expiation. This is more than just a sacrifice. This is the people of the LORD seeking to appease the LORD whom they have offended through their sins. This application of the blood is a sign of a people who are piously seeking the forgiveness of the LORD whom they have offended. This is expressed in the use of hyssop, which is used in the Scriptures in conjunction with purification or cleansing. The application of the blood, in effect, made every home an altar, holy and acceptable unto the LORD.

B. Concerning the Lamb

Exodus 12:8-11

And they shall eat the flesh in that night, roast with fire, and unleavened bread; and with bitter herbs they shall eat it. [12:9] Eat not of it raw, nor sodden at all with water, but roast with fire; his head with his legs, and with the purtenance thereof. [12:10] And ye shall let nothing of it remain until the morning; and that which remaineth of it until the morning ye shall burn with fire. [12:11] And thus shall ye eat it; with your loins girded, your shoes on your feet, and your staff in your hand; and ye shall eat it in haste: it is the LORD'S passover.

The LORD not only gives specific instructions on how the blood was to be used but He even gives specific instructions on how the lamb was to be prepared for the meal. It is to be roasted with fire and prepared with bitter herbs. Don't eat it raw, don't boil it in water, it is to be roasted with fire.

The primary reason for the lamb being roasted on the fire is so that it may be prepared without being broken apart. The entire lamb was prepared and presented upon the table without a bone being broken. The commentary of Keil and Delitzsch stated the reason for the lamb being prepared in this manner.

> *"By avoiding the breaking of the bones, the animal was preserved in complete integrity, undisturbed and entire (Psa_34:20). The sacrificial lamb to be eaten was to be thoroughly and perfectly whole, and at the time of eating was to appear as a perfect whole, and therefore as one."*

The lamb was to be prepared with bitter herbs. This is not to signify that they had herbs as a side dish but that the lamb, being roasted on the fire, would be wrapped in the bitter herbs. These herbs represented the bitterness of which the Hebrews had been subjected to as they served the Egyptians.

C. Concerning the Bread

Exodus 12:8

And they shall eat the flesh in that night, roast with fire, and unleavened bread; and with bitter herbs they shall eat it.

Exodus 12:15-20

Seven days shall ye eat unleavened bread; even the first day ye shall put away leaven out of your houses: for whosoever eateth leavened bread from the first day until the seventh day, that soul shall be cut off from Israel. [12:16] And in the first day there shall be an holy convocation, and in the seventh day there shall be an holy convocation to you; no manner of work shall be done in them, save that which every man must eat, that only may be done of you. [12:17] And ye shall observe the feast of unleavened bread; for in this selfsame day have I brought your armies out of the land of Egypt: therefore shall ye observe this day in your generations by an ordinance for ever. [12:18] In the first month, on the fourteenth day of the month at even, ye shall eat unleavened bread, until the one and twentieth day of the month at even. [12:19] Seven days shall there be no leaven found in your houses: for whosoever eateth that which is leavened, even that soul shall be cut off from the congregation of Israel, whether he be a stranger, or born in the land. [12:20] Ye shall eat nothing leavened; in all your habitations shall ye eat unleavened bread.

The LORD also sets this time as a memorial, a feast or celebration that is to be kept forever. This feast is the feast of unleavened bread. This feast begins on the fourteenth day of the month and continues until the twenty-first day of the month. It begins and ends with a holy convocation. All the Hebrews were to observe this feast and they were to attend the convocation.

Their kneading troughs are packed with the stuff and therefore they cannot make bread with yeast or leaven. The bread they are to make is unleavened. This is not pleasant bread. It is not sweet bread. It is a bread that also represents the bitterness of their years in Egypt but it also represents the haste in which they were delivered.

D. Concerning the Eating

Exodus 12:11

And thus shall ye eat it; with your loins girded, your shoes on your feet, and your staff in your hand; and ye shall eat it in haste: it is the LORD'S passover.

The LORD not only tells the Hebrew people how to apply the blood, cook the lamb, and prepare the bread; He even tells them how they are to eat the meal. They are to have their loins girded. This is symbolic of being ready to go. They wore robes and when they would go to work, they would gird their robes or tuck them into a belt. The LORD says have your loins girded.

He also says to have your shoes on your feet. When we visit a person's home it is often customary for the host or hostess to ask, may I take your coat? In the ancient customs of Rome when a person entered the home a servant would take their shoes. Even in ancient times of Egypt, it was seen as inconsiderate to eat with your shoes on. Here again the implication is that the LORD is about to deliver you and you need to be ready to go.

In the ancient days, it was very common for a traveler to carry a staff. This aided them in the journey. When the LORD says have your staff in your hand, it is another indication that you better be ready to go.

It was very customary for a meal to last several hours. It was considered rude to eat quickly and rush out. The LORD tells the Hebrews eat in haste. Yet again, another indicator that what He is about to do He is going to do quickly.

III. The Specific Promise

Exodus 12:12

For I will pass through the land of Egypt this night, and will smite all the firstborn in the land of Egypt, both man and beast; and against all the gods of Egypt I will execute judgment: I am the LORD.

Exodus 12:24-28

And ye shall observe this thing for an ordinance to thee and to thy sons for ever. [12:25] And it shall come to pass, when ye be come to the land which the LORD will give you, according as he hath promised, that ye shall keep this service. [12:26] And it shall come to pass, when your children shall say unto you, What mean ye by this service? [12:27] That ye shall say, It is the sacrifice of the LORD'S passover, who passed over the houses of the children of Israel in Egypt, when he smote the Egyptians, and delivered our houses. And the people bowed the head and worshipped. [12:28] And the children of Israel went away, and did as the LORD had commanded Moses and Aaron, so did they.

I hope you are getting a clear picture of what the LORD is saying in these verses. The LORD is saying you had better be ready because I am coming and I will deliver you this very night. I will pass through, I will smite the firstborn, and I will execute judgment because I am the LORD.

Remember that LORD represents the all-powerful, self-existent, eternal, holy, sin-hating, and covenant keeping God. The Hebrews have been in bondage to the Egyptians for four-hundred years but the LORD is still in control and He is going to deliver them this very night.

The LORD also commands that the Hebrews observe this ordinance for ever. The LORD says I want you to remember and to never forget what is about to happen on this night. The LORD reminds them of His promise to them, "when you come to the land that I will give you, the land that I promised you." The LORD says I remember my promises and I will keep them.

When you are enjoying the blessings of the land that I give you and the promise is fulfilled, you need to remember this day! This is the day that I delivered you! And when your children say why are we celebrating? Why are we roasting a lamb? Why are we eating bitter herbs and unleavened bread? Why are we eating with our shoes on and in our travelling clothes? On that day you will say, we do this because we are remembering the LORD's Passover. We are remembering how he passed over us when he smote the Egyptians. We are remembering the LORD and Jehovah is his name.

QUESTIONS

1. How do you remember when the LORD delivered you?

2. Why did the LORD give such specific instructions on when and how to celebrate?

3. How is the blood of the Passover lamb like the blood of Christ?

4. How can we show that we believe the LORD is going to keep His promises for the future?

5. In what ways are you showing your children that the LORD has kept His promises in the past?

CONCLUSION

I firmly believe that if we are going to understand the New Testament, we must have some understanding of the Old Testament. Perhaps there is no better place to begin than with understanding the plagues and the Passover.

In the plagues, we see the mercy and the long-suffering of the LORD. Pharaoh could have been spared from any of the plagues, if he would have accepted the message of the LORD. In the Passover, we also see the mercy and long-suffering of the LORD. Although his chosen people had rebelled against Him, the LORD was faithful to keep His promise to deliver them.

Many years after the Hebrews were delivered from their bondage to the Egyptians, God sent His Son to die on the cross for us. Jesus was called the Lamb of God. He was slain for our sins on the evening of the fourteenth day of the first month of the Hebrew calendar. It is through His blood that we have forgiveness of our sins. Now instead of being under the judgment of God, when God looks at us, He sees the blood of the Lamb and He passes over us.

If you have never asked the LORD to forgive you of your sins and to deliver you from the bondage that they bring, I encourage you to do so right now. It can be done as easily as these four steps:

1. Realize you have sinned against God.
Romans 3:23 says, "For all have sinned, and come short of the glory of God;"

2. Recognize where sin leads.
Romans 6:23 says, "For the wages of sin is death;"

3. Receive the Gospel.
Romans 5:8 says, "But God commendeth his love toward us, in that, while we were yet sinners, Christ died for us."

4. Repent of your sins.
Romans 10:13 says, "For whosoever shall call upon the name of the Lord shall be saved."

If you believe this, then call upon the name of the Lord in a prayer like this, "Lord, I know that I am a sinner. I believe that Christ died on the cross to pay for my sins. I ask you to forgive my sins and save me, in Jesus name, Amen."

Christians, the LORD has left us with specific instructions as to how we are to live our lives. We are not to live like those who have not experienced His deliverance. We are not to trample the blood of Christ. We are not to despise our deliverance by thinking that things were better in our bondage. The bondage of sin is bitterness, it is death, and it is destruction.

The LORD has delivered us and He has given us this promise, we will come to the land, that heavenly land, and there we shall forever be with the LORD. The LORD has promised that He will return and when He does we shall be caught up with Him. He is no slack concerning His promise. He said behold, I come quickly. Are you living a life that is prepared to go? He could come at any moment. Let us be prepared and let us tell others that Jesus is the way, the truth, and the life.

WHEN I SMITE THE LAND

BIBLIOGRAPHY

- Against All the Gods of Egypt, David Padfield, 2002, www.padfield.com
- http://www.kenseamedia.com/egyptian_gods/
- http://www.touregypt.net/
- http://www.princeton.edu/~achaney/tmve/wiki10 0k/docs/khnum.html
- http://www.britannica.com/ebchecked/topic/4224 62/nun
- http://www.kendalluk.com/sacredinsect.htm
- E-Sword
    - Adam Clarke's Commentary on the Bible
    - Albert Barnes' Notes on the Bible
    - Easton's Bible Dictionary
    - Fausset's Bible Dictionary
    - Hitchcock's Bible Names
    - International Standard Bible Encyclopedia
    - Jamieseon, Fausset, and Brown Commentary
    - John Gill's Exposition of the Entire Bible
    - Keil and Delitzsch Commentary on the Old Testament
    - Matthew Henry's Commentary on the Whole Bible
    - Smith's Bible Dictionary
    - Strong's Hebrew Concordance
    - Webster's 1828 Dictionary

ILLUSTRATIONS

- Cover Photo: By Madinpursuit (Own work) [CC0], via Wikimedia Commons (http://upload.wikimedia.org/wikipedia/commons /6/61/Sphinx_Armachi.jpg)
- Figure 1:By mask_of_amenemope_by_john_campana.jpg: (http://creativecommons.org/licenses/by/2.0), via wikimedia commons
- Figure 2: The Gods of Egypt, Volume II, E.A. Wallis Budge, 1904, Chicago, The Open Court Publishing Company, page 50.
- Figure 3: Ibid, page 42
- Figure 4: By E. A. Wallis Budge (1857-1937) (The Egyptian Religion of the Resurrection) [Public domain], via Wikimedia Commons
- Figure 5: The Gods of Egypt, Volume II, E.A. Wallis Budge, 1904, Chicago, The Open Court Publishing Company, page 30.
- Figure 6: (http://commons.wikimedia.org/wiki/file%3anun_ raises_the_sun.jpg)
- Figure 7: Roland Unger [GFDL (http://www.gnu.org/copyleft/fdl.html) or CC-BY-SA-3.0-2.5-2.0-1.0 (http://creativecommons.org/licenses/by-sa/3.0)], via Wikimedia Commons
- Figure 8: The Gods of Egypt, Volume II, E.A. Wallis Budge, 1904, Chicago, The Open Court Publishing Company, page 95.

- Figure 9: The Gods of Egypt, Volume I, E.A. Wallis Budge, 1904, London, Methuen and Company, page 440
- Figure 10: By Jeff Dahl (Own work) [GFDL (http://www.gnu.org/copyleft/fdl.html) or CC-BY-SA-3.0-2.5-2.0-1.0 (http://creativecommons.org/licenses/by-sa/3.0)], via Wikimedia Commons
- Figure 11: http://www.touregypt.net/egyptmuseum/egyptian _museumm5.htm
- Figure 12: by anonymous (loïc evanno) [gfdl (http://www.gnu.org/copyleft/fdl.html), cc-by-sa-3.0 (http://creativecommons.org/licenses/by-sa/3.0/) or cc-by-2.5 (http://creativecommons.org/licenses/by/2.5)], via wikimedia commons
- Figure 13: by drnhawkins (own work) [cc0], via wikimedia commons
- Figure 14: by jeff dahl (own work) [gfdl (http://www.gnu.org/copyleft/fdl.html) or cc-by-sa-3.0-2.5-2.0-1.0 (http://creativecommons.org/licenses/by-sa/3.0)], via wikimedia commons
- Figure 15: The Gods of Egypt, Volume II, E.A. Wallis Budge, 1904, Chicago, The Open Court Publishing Company, page 90.
- Figure 16: by jeff dahl (own work) [gfdl (http://www.gnu.org/copyleft/fdl.html) or cc-by-sa-3.0-2.5-2.0-1.0 (http://creativecommons.org/licenses/by-sa/3.0)], via wikimedia commons

- Figure 17: The Gods of Egypt, Volume II, E.A. Wallis Budge, 1904, Chicago, The Open Court Publishing Company, page 131.
- Figure 18: Ibid, frontispiece.
- Figure 19: Ibid, page 286.
- Figure 20: Ibid, page 143.

Made in the USA
Monee, IL
19 November 2024

70534217R10115